ROUTLEDGE LIBRARY EDITIONS:
ECONOMICS AND SOCIETY

Volume 25

THE PRICE LEVEL

THE PRICE LEVEL

A Further Problem in National Planning

K. E. EDGEWORTH

Routledge
Taylor & Francis Group
LONDON AND NEW YORK

First published in 1935 by George Allen & Unwin Ltd.

This edition first published in 2026
by Routledge
4 Park Square, Milton Park, Abingdon, Oxon OX14 4RN

and by Routledge
605 Third Avenue, New York, NY 10158

Routledge is an imprint of the Taylor & Francis Group, an informa business

British Library Cataloguing in Publication Data
A catalogue record for this book is available from the British Library

ISBN: 978-1-032-97576-4 (Set)
ISBN: 978-1-041-14456-4 (Volume 25) (hbk)
ISBN: 978-1-041-14462-5 (Volume 25) (pbk)
ISBN: 978-1-003-67452-8 (Volume 25) (ebk)

DOI: 10.4324/9781003674528

THE PRICE LEVEL

A FURTHER PROBLEM IN NATIONAL PLANNING

by

LIEUT.-COLONEL K. E. EDGEWORTH
D.S.O., M.C., A.M.I.E.E.

LONDON
GEORGE ALLEN & UNWIN LTD
MUSEUM STREET

FIRST PUBLISHED IN GREAT BRITAIN IN 1935

Printed in Great Britain by
NEILL & CO., LTD., EDINBURGH

PREFACE

THIS essay continues the examination of the monetary system which was commenced in the author's earlier essay *The Trade Balance*.

In regard to the scope of our inquiry, it may be well to explain that, although a complete programme of national planning must necessarily include the development of an adequate and efficient monetary system, the development of an ideal monetary system will not in itself provide a solution to certain national problems which are also of urgent importance at the present time. No reference will be made therefore to the problem of decaying industries and distressed areas, for the reason that this problem involves the adoption of measures of a different type to those with which we are immediately concerned. Nor will any attempt be made to review the various factors which influence the distribution of wealth between capital and labour: that also is another story. The author may return to these matters on some future occasion.

For the moment we are concerned with monetary problems, and the author's analysis has led to the conclusion that such mechanisms as may have existed during the nineteenth century for controlling the trade balance and the price level have failed to carry out their functions under the more exacting conditions of the present day. If an attempt is made to revert to a monetary system based on a fixed gold standard or on a system of fixed exchanges, disequilibrium between the monetary positions in different countries is sure to arise sooner or later, from one cause or another, and must lead to a fresh financial crisis and further restriction of international trade.

At the present time there are two fundamental monetary problems to be solved. Firstly, there is the problem of restoring equilibrium between the different national monetary systems, and secondly, there is the problem of devising an international monetary system which will not contain within itself the seeds of its own destruction.

The first of these problems will probably be solved by the devaluation of those currencies which are still based on gold, and the great danger is that people will be led to believe that some such development can be regarded as a final settlement of the whole business. Nothing could in fact be further from the truth. It is the second problem, the problem of designing a new international monetary system which will really meet the needs of the present day, which should be treated as the vital issue, and this issue should not be obscured or compromised by attempts to secure the temporary relief which would follow the restoration of monetary equilibrium.

The experience of the nineteenth century has shown that the art of management, properly applied, is capable of mitigating the intensity of the fluctuations which occur in an unmanaged system, and the inference to be drawn from this experience is that the solution of our problem lies in the direction of further developing the art of management. Nor is there much difficulty in defining the objectives which should guide the governing body in the exercise of its functions. It would no doubt be generally agreed that the ideal monetary system should aim at securing the following results:—

Firstly, the expansion of trade and industry should be facilitated by an ample supply of cheap money, and should be restricted only when there are signs of over-trading and the development of boom conditions.

Secondly, violent fluctuations in the activity of trade should be avoided as far as possible.

Thirdly, there should be adequate control of the trade balance without excessive restriction of international trade.

Fourthly, the price level should be reasonably stable, particularly over the long period.

But is it possible to devise a monetary system which will be consistent in itself and which will secure all these perhaps divergent objectives? The author believes that it is, and the purpose of these essays is to indicate the general character of the solution.

My thanks are due to Dr. George O'Brien, Professor of Economics in University College, Dublin, for checking the manuscript and for a number of helpful criticisms.

K. E. E.

July 1935.

CONTENTS

THE PRICE LEVEL

CHAPTER I

INTRODUCTION

THE ELEMENTARY THEORY OF PRICES

THE elementary theory of prices as applied to individual business transactions is a simple and straightforward matter. The quantity of any article which people will buy depends to some extent on the price at which is is offered for sale. If the price is reduced people will buy more, and if it is raised people will buy less. Whatever may be the conditions which determine the supply therefore, there will usually be a particular price at which demand will be equal to supply. Moreover, if the remuneration which the producers receive in any particular occupation is less than they would receive elsewhere, there will be a tendency for the workers to transfer themselves from those industries which are less profitable to those which are more so.

It appears at first sight therefore that the price mechanism is a device which is capable of bringing about, not only an automatic adjustment between supply and demand, but also an automatic adjustment between wages in one industry and wages in another. In practice, however, matters are by no means so simple, and complications arise which are of two distinct kinds.

In the first place, it is found that both supply and demand are often inflexible, that the transfer of labour from one industry to another may be a matter, not of months nor of years, but rather of decades, and that the natural process of adjustment which has been referred to above is very slow and inefficient in practice. How to facilitate this process of readjustment is one problem.

In the second place, it is found that changes occur, not only in the prices of particular products, but also in the general level of prices in the country as a whole, and these changes in the price level cause serious reactions which interfere with the smooth working of the economic machine. How to avoid or reduce these disturbances is another problem, and it is to this latter problem rather than the former that the reader's attention is invited in the present essay.

THE MONETARY SYSTEM OF THE NINETEENTH CENTURY

The price level is only one of the factors which enter into the composition of the monetary system, and to some extent a discussion of the price level is necessarily a discussion of the monetary system as a whole.

The nineteenth century witnessed the gradual development of an international monetary system which continued to discharge its functions with reasonable efficiency until the outbreak of the Great War, and the achievements of this system furnish the natural starting-point for any discussion of the subject.

Perhaps the most interesting thing about the system was that it was not really an international system in the literal sense of the words at all. The basis of the whole system was the sterling bill of exchange, and it was the confidence with which this instrument was accepted in every important country in the world which gave to the system its essentially international character. (1)

It was necessary for the smooth working of the system that the bills representing the flow of trade in one direction should cancel those which represented the flow in the opposite direction, and that this result was actually attained in practice was due to certain special features of the system itself. Modern writers often refer to managed currencies as if the management of money were a new idea, and this practice has tended to obscure the historical fact that the international monetary system of the nineteenth century was in fact a managed currency, managed with considerable skill and success by the Bank of England and the London Money Market. It is this fact which entitles one to say that the whole system was a sterling system rather than an international system, for there was never any suggestion that other authorities should be invited to co-operate with the Bank of England in reaching decisions on matters of monetary policy.

The true significance of the whole system has been further obscured by the common practice of referring to it as the gold standard, for this title lays undue emphasis on what is after all only one aspect of a very complex piece of economic mechanism. The fact that the sterling bill was payable in gold was an essential, but by no means the only essential, feature of the whole business.

After the Great War an attempt was made to restore this international monetary system, and it appeared at first sight as if the attempt would prove successful, for there was a general expansion of trade and industry. This temporary improvement was succeeded, however, by a general collapse from which the world has not yet recovered. Many causes no doubt contributed to this disaster, but a general misunderstanding of the monetary problem was certainly not one of the least important. Undue emphasis was laid on a return to the gold standard, and the even greater importance of restoring the central control was entirely overlooked.

As matters now stand we are compelled to ask whether the restoration of the nineteenth century monetary system is possible, and if it is possible whether it is desirable. Further, if its restoration is not possible or desirable, what new system can be devised to take its place?

THE ORTHODOX POSITION

There are a number of British economists, belonging to what may conveniently be called the extreme orthodox school of economic thought, who believe that a fresh attempt should be made to restore the monetary system of the nineteenth century, a system which is often somewhat loosely described as the gold standard. The supporters of this doctrine can point to the fact that the system worked with tolerable efficiency for the best part of a century, and that no alternative system has stood the test of experience. They are further able to show that governments adopted policies which were inconsistent with the proper working of the system, and they argue that these acts are largely responsible for our present troubles. (2)

The author's criticism of this position falls under four main heads.

Firstly, efficient management by the Bank of England in conjunction with the London money market was an essential feature of the system, and without such management the system is not workable. Management of the international currency system by the Bank of England was rendered possible by the existence of certain conditions which no longer hold good and which cannot be restored.

Secondly, if it is suggested that the duty of management could be undertaken by an international bank, such as the Bank of International Settlements, the answer is that the nations of the world are not agreed as to the correct objectives of international monetary policy nor are they prepared to endow any international body with the powers which would be necessary to render the control effective.

Thirdly, the advocates of the gold standard admit that a flexible price level is necessary for the proper working of the system, and consider that steps should be taken to render prices and wages more flexible. The author is not prepared to concede that a flexible price level or flexible wages are either necessary or desirable.

Fourthly, the orthodox method of dealing with an adverse trade balance is to restrict credit in the hope that a trade depression will lower prices. The author is not prepared to agree that restriction of credit is ever admissible unless there are reasons for suspecting over-trading.

THE ACTIVITY OF TRADE

The activity of trade is a convenient phrase whereby to describe a factor in the economic situation which is measured by the proportion of potential wage-earners who are in active employment, and it would no doubt be generally agreed that the activity of trade is a matter of vital consequence to the community as a whole and to wage-earners in particular; but it is necessary I think to go further than this. It is necessary to recognise that, of all the economic factors which affect the welfare of the community, the activity of trade is the most important. As regards fluctuations in the activity of trade, it will be noted that the occurrence of such fluctuations must necessarily reduce the average proportion of employment, and it is therefore clear that our objective, as above defined, includes the reduction and control of excessive fluctuations, but it also emphasises the point that the control of the fluctuations is not the whole of our objective but only a part. The postition may be summed up by saying that:—

The primary objective of economic policy should be the control of the activity of trade in such a manner as to secure the employment of a high proportion of potential wage-earners.

In adopting this attitude it is not intended to suggest that the trade balance and the price level are not also factors of importance, far from it. But the point which it is desired to bring out is that they are not in themselves so important as the activity of trade. It may rather be said that it is the fact that the trade balance and the price level react upon the activity of trade that lends to these factors such importance as they actually possess. If the economic structure is to be viewed in its true perspective, the activity of trade should occupy the foreground, and the trade balance and the price level should be relegated to the middle distance.

The way in which recent theory and practice have gone astray is this. The nineteenth century produced one and only one instrument of management —the bank rate—and this instrument of management was originally used for controlling the activity of trade, a purpose for which it was eminently fitted. But as time went on difficulties were experienced with the trade balance and the price level and the currency authority was compelled to use the only instrument at its disposal—the bank rate—for controlling these factors also. Other possible methods of control were "taboo," and manipulation of the gold parity or the exchange rates were regarded as devices which were not quite respectable. Theory simply followed in the wake of practice and endeavoured to explain how the system was actually able to work.

The recent crisis in its various phases has brought out very clearly the weakness of a system which attempts to employ a single instrument of management for the control of three separate factors, and has shown how essential it is that the whole system of management should be reviewed and reconstructed to meet the more exacting requirements of the present day.

The question of devising additional instruments will be dealt with in due course. In the meantime the argument of the present section may be summarised as follows:—

The activity of trade is of greater importance than any other factor in the economic structure, and the management of credit is the correct and appropriate instrument for con-

trolling the activity of trade, and the effectiveness of this instrument should not be impaired by attempting to use it for any other purpose.

THE TRADE BALANCE

It has long been recognised that the ebb and flow of gold together with the price fluctuations which are produced by these gold movements tend to bring about a balance between imports and exports, and, during the nineteenth century, this automatic mechanism was relied on to bring about the necessary control of the trade balance.

In the decade following the Great War the mechanism failed to act, and this failure was one of the major causes of the great depression. In the world of to-day countries are no longer able to leave the trade balance to adjust itself, but they have been compelled, not only to realise the importance of balancing imports against exports, but to adopt all sorts of emergency expedients in order to secure the necessary measure of control.

The general effect of these policies has been to impede and restrict international trade, which has dwindled to a mere fraction of its former volume, and this restriction has led in turn to a great deal of unemployment and distress.

A few enthusiasts have gone so far as to express a belief that exchange control should be regarded as a permanent feature of the economic system, but this view is not shared by traders and economists in general. Something much more flexible is required if international prosperity is to be restored.

The writer has discussed elsewhere this problem of balancing imports and exports and has pointed out that the proper and appropriate instrument for the control of the trade balance is a variable gold parity (or variable exchange), and he has examined the conditions under which such a system should be operated. (3)

For our immediate purpose the important point to note is the relationship which necessarily exists between policy in regard to the trade balance and policy in regard to the price level. If we follow the orthodox school and regard changes in the price level as part of the normal mechanism for controlling the trade balance, then stabilisation, or indeed any other considered policy in regard to the price level, can never be more than the expression of a pious hope. It is only when a distinct and independent system of control is established for the trade balance that it becomes possible to regard stabilisation, or any other definite policy in regard to the price level, as a practical possibility.

In entering upon our discussion of the price level therefore, it is necessarily assumed that an independent control for the trade balance has been established and is in successful operation, so that the internal price level will be free from the pressure which is necessarily produced by any serious excess of either imports or exports.

THE STABILISATION OF PRICES

The orthodox policy referred to in an earlier section is not the only economic policy which has gained supporters; there are other policies which have been favoured by professional economists and other writers. One popular idea, for example, is represented by the suggestion that monetary policy should be directed towards the stabilisation of prices, but there are two more or less distinct schools of thought by which this proposal is supported.

What may be called the British school proposes that prices should be stabilised by an appropriate manipulation of credit, while the American school pins its faith to changes in the gold parity of the currency.

It is unnecessary to anticipate the detailed discussion which will be found in later chapters of this essay, but the author may summarise his criticism of these two schools as follows:—

Firstly, it is not sufficiently recognised that the policy of stabilising prices is inconsistent with the normal working of the nineteenth-century gold standard. To be consistent, those who advocate stable prices must abandon the orthodox attitude towards the trade balance and must disclose some new and unorthodox method of dealing with that particular problem of control.

Secondly, it is not sufficiently recognised that the power of any known form of control is limited both in regard to its extent and in regard to the speed with which it acts. Claims are made that a policy of price stabilisation would secure results which are in fact quite unattainable in practice.

Thirdly, neither the management of credit as suggested by the British school nor changes in the gold parity as suggested by the American school are in fact appropriate instruments for the control of the price level. The former exerts a direct influence on the activity of trade and the latter a direct influence on the trade balance, but neither causes any direct effect on the price level.

These arguments will be further elaborated in due course.

A MORE GENERAL THEORY

It would no doubt be generally agreed that any serious maladjustment in the economic machine may provoke reactions which are liable to spread in various directions and which may influence other factors besides those which were originally responsible for the disturbance. It is also true that disturbances of abnormal intensity are usually due to a number of separate factors which happen to be acting in unison. Nevertheless these considerations do not bind together the various factors sufficiently closely to justify us in regarding them as different aspects of a single variable.

If an engineer finds that one of his machines is suffering from excessive vibration he does not expect to be able to effect a cure by the application of some universal panacea. He analyses the cause or causes of the vibration and for each separate cause he devises a distinct and appropriate remedy. If the economist is to be successful he must do the same; he must analyse each distinct type of disturbance and he must then devise an appropriate remedy for each particular case. In fact we may say:—

Under modern conditions the smooth working of the economic machine depends upon a number of separate factors which operate to some extent independently of one another and any one of which may require separate control.

Of the factors referred to the three most important are the activity of trade, the trade balance and the price level. There are of course others, in fact they are legion, but these three are fundamental and demand our special consideration.

Now the engineer, having found that the vibrations in his machine were of three distinct kinds due to three distinct causes, would not expect to find a single remedy for such a condition of affairs. He might be lucky and find a comprehensive remedy, but he would certainly not regard the discovery of a comprehensive remedy as inevitable. What he would expect to find would be that separate and distinct remedies would have to be devised to meet each of his three difficulties. The author's view is that economic troubles should be dealt with on the same principle, that is to say:—

Every economic factor which requires control needs a separate and appropriate instrument of management by means of which control may be exercised.

Once the truth of this proposition is realised, many recent errors in the art of management are made clear, and the barrenness of much economic controversy is exposed, for it immediately becomes evident that the bank rate might perhaps be used (if it can be shown to be suitable) for the control of the activity of trade or for the control of the trade balance or for the control of the price level, but it cannot reasonably be expected to control two of these factors at the same time, and still less can it be expected to control all three.

THE SYSTEM OF THE FUTURE

The considerations which have been set forth above lead to the view that monetary management in the future will comprise at least three distinct branches:—

Firstly, the control of the activity of trade, for which the appropriate instrument of management is the bank rate. This is the original purpose for which the bank rate was first used, and there is ample experience to show that it can be effectively employed for that purpose.

Secondly, the control of the trade balance. The author has discussed this problem elsewhere and has reached the conclusion that the appropriate instrument of management is a variable gold parity or variable exchange.

Thirdly, the control of the price level, which is the subject of investigation in the present essay.

CHAPTER II

THE TIME FACTOR

ITS IMPORTANCE

Nearly all phenomena take time for their accomplishment, and the reactions with which we are concerned in our study of economics can seldom be regarded as instantaneous in operation. Months elapse between seed time and harvest, and there is a further delay while the wheat is transported to its ultimate destination and converted into bread.

Again, when the construction of factories, the sinking of mine shafts and similar activities are under consideration, the time lag between cause and effect is even greater and is to be reckoned in terms of years rather than in months or weeks.

All this is well known, and yet, perhaps because the influence of the time factor is not easy to define with precision, no accepted method of introducing time into the study of economic problems has been developed. The lapse of time between cause and effect is often referred to, but as often as not it is forgotten, and much slipshod reasoning and false argument is the result of this neglect.

The discussion of practical problems always necessitates the use of special assumptions designed to simplify the analysis and avoid unnecessary complications, but it is essential that these simplifying assumptions should be legitimate in themselves, and that we should be in a position to estimate the extent of the error which is involved in their adoption. We are not entitled to ignore essential factors merely because they give rise to difficulties in our theoretical investigations.

A TYPICAL EXAMPLE

The difficulties with which economic problems are surrounded and the way in which errors of the type referred to are liable to creep in may be conveniently illustrated by means of a well-known example.

We begin by defining economic profit as the difference between cost and selling price. We may represent these three quantities by symbols, and we may express their relationship by means of an equation of the form:—

$$A = B - C$$

Moreover, we may add dignity to our equation by calling it an identity and by suggesting that, if our definitions are properly framed, the equation cannot fail to be true.

Let us look into the matter a little more carefully, however.

If an equation is to be an identity, then each of the quantities which enter into it must have an exact meaning. If our equation is to provide us with a means of calculating the quantity we have called profit, then the other two quantities which enter into the equation must be so defined that they possess precise values.

Consider first the question of selling price. Suppose that a customer goes into a baker's shop and buys a loaf of bread, then the price of the loaf has clearly a definite value. But if a merchant in London buys a consignment of coffee from a producer in Brazil the transaction cannot be said to exhibit the same precise character. We have to consider whether the sale is to be regarded as taking place at the moment when the coffee leaves Brazil or at the moment when it arrives in London, and the price which is paid will differ according to the decision which is arrived at, for in the interval money must be regarded as earning interest.

When we turn to the question of costs the position is even more complex. The baker has to meet certain fixed charges and the appropriate fraction of these charges must be debited to such individual loaf. The baker's output, however, is not fixed; it may vary from day to day, and we must decide whether the fixed charges are to be averaged over the daily output, the weekly output or the annual output. In actual fact the usual practice is to work out an annual balance sheet, and it is only when this account has been completed that a definite figure can be assigned to the cost of the individual loaf. Moreover, since the cost thus arrived at is an average cost, the cost of the loaf sold in January may be influenced by something which does not take place until the following December. Nor can we evade the issue by assuming that a daily balance sheet is prepared, for there are specific costs which are only incurred at stated intervals and which must be averaged over the periods to which they refer.

This kind of discussion could of course be continued indefinitely, but enough has I hope been said to reveal the absurdities which are involved in the assumption that the cost and selling price of any article are quantities which have precise values at any given instant of time.

The idea of economic profit is a very useful one which can be made to play an important part in our study of business relationships, but its value will be destroyed if we assume that it has an exact value for each individual transaction and that the quantities thus defined provide suitable material for mathematical manipulation.

It is essential to realise that the preparation of accounts and statistics is not instantaneous, and that there is a time lag between the actual business transactions and the reactions which they ultimately call forth.

MONETARY FALLACIES

We shall find in due course that monetary problems involve a large number of factors, and that the nature of the relationships between these quantities is neither uniform nor simple.

It follows that such problems cannot be adequately stated in terms of elementary mathematical equations, and that any attempt to express them in this form imposes limitations which involve the omission of factors which are actually of practical importance and the introduction of simplified relationships which do not coincide with the facts.

It is not necessary to discuss the various pseudo-mathematical theories which have been put forward in greater detail, since the reader who is interested in the matter can easily test them for himself. It is a simple matter to examine any particular theory of the price level and tabulate the factors which have actually been allowed for and those which have been omitted. Nor is it difficult to compare the assumed relationship between the various quantities with those which are known to exist in practice.

In the unlikely event of a theory passing these two elementary tests, a further test must be made before it can be accepted as valid.

The various assumptions made in the course of the argument must be examined to ascertain whether they are always true or whether they are true for the short, the medium or the long period only. As a result of this examination it may transpire that all the assumptions are true for medium periods of time, and in that case the final result is true for the medium period only. On the other hand, it is much more likely that some of the assumptions made are true for the short period only, others for the medium period only, and yet others for the long period only. In that case the whole argument is evidently fallacious and must be rejected.

The writer has not so far become acquainted with any precise formulæ which will satisfy these simple tests, and he must confess that it appears to him unlikely that any complete and precise theory will be formulated in the near future.

In the meantime it is necessary to discuss the whole problem in general terms and to employ such methods of reasoning as may seem to be appropriate in each particular case.

STATICAL AND DYNAMICAL PROBLEMS

The elementary theory of mechanics is divided into statics and dynamics, and no qualified engineer would be likely to fall into the error of attempting to solve a dynamical problem by means of statical equations. And yet this is precisely what economists always seem to be trying to do.

The economic structure of the modern world is inherently unstable, and many of the practical problems which we are called upon to solve are essentially dynamic in character, and yet solutions are constantly offered in the form of statical equations embellished with much elaboration of detail. Correct results cannot possibly be obtained by such methods.

It may happen that there will come a day when our knowledge of economic processes is such that the way in which time enters into our problems can be precisely defined, and a formal mathematical analysis of the position will then be possible. In the meantime one has to be content with other methods.

It is often the practice of writers on economics to qualify some statement by saying that it is true for the long period or the short period or whatever it may be, and this type of expression indicates a method of approach which can claim a more serious logical basis than is perhaps generally attributed to it.

PERIODIC AND QUASI-PERIODIC DISTURBANCES

Absolutely rigid structures are unknown to us. All the structures with which we are acquainted possess the properties of flexibility and inertia, and the combined effect of these two properties is that the structures themselves exhibit effects of a periodic or quasi-periodic character.

In many cases the structure exhibits the property of resonance and tends to vibrate at some particular frequency or frequencies. Sometimes, and certain atomic structures may be quoted as examples, the resonance is so sharp that it transcends our power of measuring it; in other cases the resonant frequency is less clearly defined. It is known that economic disturbances do exhibit periodic characteristics, but attempts to determine precise periods have not been conspicuously successful. It is not to be expected that they would be, for the factors on which the frequency of these disturbances must depend are evidently not constant. Progress in the theory of these phenomena will not be achieved by searching for oscillations of a precisely periodic character, but rather by a careful study of the general character of the mechanism and by the development of statistical methods which will enable the importance of particular factors to be estimated.

This well-known property of resonance is not, however, the one with which we are immediately concerned; there is another less-known property of oscillatory systems which is of special importance in connection with our present investigation, and the theory of this particular effect has been developed to a considerable extent in connection with what are known to the electrical engineer as "filters."

These structures are of various types. An arrangement known as a high pass filter will have a certain resistance at frequencies below its critical frequency, then, as the critical frequency is approached, the resistance falls more or less abruptly, and finally, at frequencies above the critical frequency, the resistance settles down to a very much lower value. Again, there is an arrangement known as a band pass filter which has a certain resistance for periods between shall we say one thousandth of a second and five thousandths of a second, and a much higher resistance for impulses of longer or shorter duration. When discussing the properties of such a structure we may call any period of time less than one thousandth part of a second a short period, any period between one thousandth and five thousandths of a second a medium period, and any period exceeding five thousandths of a second a long period, and we may say that certain rules hold good for the medium period but that different rules must be framed to describe what happens in short or long periods.

Now the point of the analogy is this. It shows that, when we are dealing with complex phenomena of a quasi-periodic character, we may expect to find that, for certain periods of time, certain factors will be of predominating importance and the phenomena will be governed by a particular set of rules. On the other hand, when we fix our attention on shorter or longer periods of time we must expect to find that a different set of factors has come into prominence and that the rules by which the phenomena are described must be modified accordingly.

When the economist says that so and so is true for, say, the long period his method of approach is perfectly logical and correct provided that the meaning of the long period is adequately defined. Until some more precise method of dealing with the time factor is available, the method of making separate analyses for short, medium and long periods of time, or whatever it may be, appears to be perfectly reasonable and appropriate.

At the same time one must condemn forms of theory which ignore the time factor and which put forward as universal laws statements which are in fact applicable only within a strictly limited field.

SHORT, MEDIUM AND LONG PERIODS

The author is fully aware that the method of introducing the time factor into our discussion of economic problems which has been described above is very far from ideal, and that the special assumptions which are now to be made are also open to criticism. Our object, however, is to gain a general insight into the working of the monetary machine, and this is not possible if the time factor is ignored. All that can be claimed is that no more comprehensive procedure appears to be available and that the method adopted seems to be adequate for our purpose.

Our analysis will be divided under three heads dealing with short, medium and long periods respectively. It is of course understood that it is impossible to draw any hard and fast lines between the short and medium periods on the one hand and the medium and long periods on the other, but the following statements will serve to indicate the order of magnitude of the quantities involved:—

(i) Periods of time of six months or less will be referred to as "short."

(ii) Periods of time between one and three years will be referred to as "medium."

(iii) Periods of time exceeding five years will be referred to as "long."

In introducing this special convention for the purpose of the present essay, however, it is perhaps desirable to warn the reader that no such convention has been generally adopted by other writers. When the expression "short period," "medium period" or "long period" occurs in the course of an economic argument therefore, it is necessary to determine, from the context, what precise meaning is to be attached to these expressions in each particular case.

CHAPTER III

VALUES AND PRICES

SOME FUNDAMENTAL DIFFICULTIES

In so far as we are concerned with the value of different things at the same time and place, the price at which anything is sold is sufficient indication of its value, or to be more precise its value in exchange. It is only when it is found necessary to compare the value of things at different times and in different places that we become aware that prices are by no means a reliable standard of value. The most which can be said of the price of any article is that it represents the ratio between the value of the article and the value of money. In order to arrive at an understanding as to what is happening, it is clearly necessary to study the factors which influence the value of money as well as those which influence the value of commodities, and it would be of great assistance to us in our investigation if we could define an absolute standard of value which would enable us to discriminate between the two different factors which combine together to produce the changes in prices which are actually found to take place.

Now while the idea of value is one of the most fundamental conceptions in the theory of economics, it is unfortunately the case that no satisfactory definition of value has yet been evolved. Adam

Smith took corn as his standard of value, while Ricardo proposed that the unit of value should be the value of the daily output of one labourer. Both these writers assumed that the idea of value could be exactly defined and measured.

Since the time of Adam Smith and Ricardo some progress has been made, but we seem to be as far from a precise conception of value as ever; rather may it be said that we have been driven to accept the view that no exact definition of value is possible and that any practical measure of value must be in the nature of an approximation. Subject to these modern reservations the two fundamental ideas discussed by Adam Smith and Ricardo still remain to us and may be described as the "commodity standard of value" and the "labour standard of value" respectively.

GOLD AND SILVER AS STANDARDS OF VALUE

Any commodity can be regarded as a standard of value and the precious metals possess certain inherent advantages for this purpose which are not shared by commodities in general, that is to say they are indestructible, the supply is not subject to seasonable fluctuations and they are of high intrinsic value. The latter consideration is of importance because it enables them to be used as money and thereby ensures that the prices of other commodities shall conform to the standard. With other standards there is always the difficulty that a special mechanism must be provided in order to prevent the value of money from diverging from the value of the accepted standard.

Nevertheless, gold and silver possess the disadvantage, which is shared by commodities in general, that the price is influenced by lack of balance between supply and demand, and changes may occur in these factors which may prove to be of serious importance. To some extent price fluctuations are modified by the fact that a higher price for the metal makes production more profitable and output is increased accordingly, but this reaction is not sufficiently rapid to ensure that values shall remain reasonably constant.

A COMMODITY STANDARD OF VALUE

The price of any commodity may be affected by lack of balance between supply and demand, and the price of some commodities such as wheat may be affected by weather conditions and by permanent changes in the efficiency of production. Some of the difficulty which thus arises can be removed by adopting as our standard of value, not the price of a single commodity, but a figure representing a combined price for a selection of different commodities. The development of these *Index Numbers*, as they are called, is perhaps the most important advance in the theory of value since the days of Adam Smith and Ricardo.

The actual index number is usually a ratio between

the average price of the selected sample on the date in question and the price on some standard date, and this form of expression is not without significance, for it involves the tacit admission that the index number is not an absolute measure of value at all. We may talk as if an index number were based on some particular standard of value, but it is in fact merely a comparison between a set of prices on one date and a corresponding set of prices on another.

The selection of the items which go to make up a particular index number and the weight to be attached to each item are of course matters of considerable importance, and we have in practice a variety of index numbers each of which has its special significance for some particular purpose. So far as the theory of value is concerned, it seems natural to identify "the commodity price level" with the retail prices at which the final products are sold to the consumer, and for the purpose of our discussion "the commodity price level" will be used in that sense. We need not concern ourselves too closely with the problem of identifying this theoretical expression with any particular index number; it is sufficient to know that index numbers can be devised which can be regarded as reasonable approximations.

A LABOUR STANDARD OF VALUE

Ricardo regarded the labour unit of value as the value of the daily output of one worker, but in attempting to attach a precise meaning to this definition it is necessary to include both indirect labour and the labour involved in creating the instruments of production.

Some early writers assumed that only direct labour need be considered, but it is clear that such a method of treatment does not correspond with the facts. Transport workers, doctors and so on are just as necessary for efficient production as the workers who are directly employed.

A further difficulty arises in regard to the labour which is employed in creating the instruments of production, for in this case the useful life of the factories and machines must enter into our calculations. Moreover, if cost price in the ordinary business meaning of the term is to be made use of in order to provide a measure of the labour employed in the course of production, the question of interest on capital intrudes itself upon our notice.

These difficulties are of the same type as those which have already been discussed in regard to the commodity standard, and they effectually prevent us from regarding any form of labour standard as an absolute measure of value. The difficulties can be somewhat reduced by fixing our attention, not on the individual worker, but on the nation as a whole, and by defining the unit of value as the national output divided by the total number of workers, but such a unit can hardly be identified with anything which can be measured in practice.

For practical purposes we must be content with a wages standard of value rather than a labour standard, and it must be represented by an index number defined as the ratio between the average rates of wages on the date in question and the average rate on some standard date.

THE EFFICIENCY OF PRODUCTION

Increasing knowledge makes possible the production of a greater quantity of commodities for a given amount of effort. Plant breeding leads to better yields from the soil, the use of machinery gives larger production from the factories, improved organisation eliminates wasted effort, and so on. All these factors combine to increase what may be called the efficiency of production. Now it is this continual increase in the efficiency of production which causes a continual divergence between the commodity and the labour standards of value, and in discussing prices it is necessary to take careful note of this divergence.

As regards actual figures, it has been estimated that the increase in the efficiency of production during the decade following the War was at the rate of about 2 per cent. per annum. Since the commencement of the depression progress has been arrested and the efficiency of production has declined.

INTERNATIONAL ASPECTS OF VALUE

The conceptions of value which have been set out above are essentially national standards and it is necessary to consider how far they are also of international significance. Or to put the question somewhat differently, how far do the artificial boundaries which are erected at the national frontiers affect the standards which we have endeavoured to set up?

We may perhaps begin by noting that the national standards are themselves merely averages, and that in different localities there may be found to exist differences both in rates of wages and in the prices of commodities. Inside the national boundaries, however, forces are in existence which work for uniformity and which tend to minimise differences. Labour tends to migrate into trades and localities in which there are higher rates of pay, and this tendency reduces inequalities in wages, while improvements in transport, the use of branded goods and the development of multiple shops are influences which tend to produce uniformity in commodity prices.

In the international field similar forces are at work but they act much more slowly, and the differences to be found between one country and another are therefore much greater than those which exist between different parts of the same country.

For the purpose of comparing values as between

one country and another an international money standard such as that which existed during the nineteenth century is evidently the most reliable, for gold costs little to transport, and it provides a standard of value which is nearly the same in all places, although it may vary considerably at different times.

Commodities in general cost more to transport than gold and silver, and, even apart from complications due to tariffs, they provide a less satisfactory international standard of value than gold or silver when the question at issue is a comparison between immediate values at different places.

Finally when we come to compare rates of wages we find, as we should expect, that the divergences between one country and another may be very great indeed. From a world-wide standpoint a labour standard of value cannot be said to be of any real significance.

THE THREE STANDARDS COMPARED

If we accept the apparently unavoidable conclusion that the search for an absolute standard of value is futile, the position as regards the three standards of value already referred to may be summarised as follows:—

There are two distinct standards of value which are of theoretical importance, namely, the commodity standard and the wages standard, and in each case changes in money value can be represented by an index number which is the ratio between the prices of a selected sample on two different dates. The reciprocal of the index number is the change in the value of money as compared with the standard.

The two standards tend to diverge owing to changes in the efficiency of production, but neither standard can be said to have any *a priori* claim to be regarded as superior to the other. Ultimately we shall find, however, that there are certain advantages to be found in stabilising commodity prices rather than wages, and we have already noted that a commodity standard is of greater international significance. For these reasons it would appear that the commodity standard of value can claim to possess the balance of advantages.

Turning to metallic standards, we note the important point that gold and silver can be used as money and that their use for that purpose provides a means for compelling prices to adhere to the standard. We further note that they can be regarded as providing a reliable and satisfactory test of value for comparing prices at different places at the same time, and that they may be accepted as a standard for that purpose provided that the metal is allowed to move freely without restriction. On the other hand, when it is a question of comparing prices at one epoch with those at another, gold and silver standards must be rejected as being very far from satisfactory.

We conclude that gold and silver may be regarded

as convenient temporary standards for comparing values at one place with those at another, but that the commodity and wages standards must be regarded as possessing a much higher degree of significance when it comes to a question of comparing values at different epochs of time.

SOME EXAMPLES

It is not the purpose of the present essay to discuss the methods which might be employed with a view to securing a more uniform distribution of wealth, but it is necessary to reject any policies which might prejudice the position of the wage-earner. It becomes necessary therefore that we should guard against any undesirable result of this character which might arise from ambiguity in regard to the standard of value, and reference will now be made to some examples which may serve to clarify the position.

Assume, in the first place, that wages are constant and that prices are constant except in so far as definite improvements are made in methods of production. If now important improvements are made in the production of some particular article, the price of that article will fall in due course, and then everybody will be in a position to purchase a larger quantity of commodities than they were before, so that both wage-earner and capitalist will benefit by increases in the efficiency of production.

As regards the trend of commodity prices, it is clear that the items which have fallen in price will effect the general result and that index numbers will fall. What we have in effect assumed is that prices have been attached to the labour unit of value, and that the increased efficiency of production has led to a fall in the prices of commodities.

We hear a good deal nowadays about stabilisation of prices, and as a second example let it be assumed that prices move in such a way that the commodity index remains stable.

If we further assume that wages are fixed it is clear that the wage-earner derives no benefit from the increased efficiency of production. In other words, fixed wages and stable prices involve changes in the distribution of the national income, changes which are to the advantage of the capitalist and to the detriment of the wage-earner. If this difficulty is to be avoided stabilisation of commodity prices must be associated with rising wages, the rate of increase being not less than the corresponding increase in the efficiency of production. Discussions on the stabilisation of commodity prices often overlook this important point.

CHAPTER IV

THE QUESTION OF POLICY

THE EFFECTS PRODUCED BY CHANGING PRICES

CHANGING prices give rise to four important effects :—

Firstly, they influence the volume of money which is necessary in connection with any given volume of business transactions.

Secondly, they alter the nature of the contracts which have been entered into between debtor and creditor, including those which arise in connection with the issue of government loans and with debentures, mortgages and other fixed charges on industry.

Thirdly, they affect the distribution of wealth as between capitalist and wage-earner.

Fourthly, rising prices give rise to windfall profits in trade, while falling prices cause losses.

The first of these effects will be referred to in subsequent chapters when we come to discuss the quantity theory of money; the other three effects are dealt with below.

DEBTOR AND CREDITOR

A borrower undertakes to pay a lender a certain rate of interest and undertakes further that he will repay the capital after a certain lapse of time, and, in making such a contract, both borrower and lender make the tacit assumption that the value of money will remain constant. If prices fall, however, the debtor finds that, although the money value of his debt remains the same, he is actually compelled to produce a larger volume of goods in order to discharge it, and he claims, not without reason, that such a result is unjust and inequitable. This aspect of the matter has been largely responsible for recent attempts to raise prices in the United States.

In a general way, then, we conclude that the value of money should remain constant. When we attempt to attach an exact meaning to this formula, however, we come up against the problem of value which has already been discussed in the previous chapter, and it is found to be impossible to offer an exact solution. The most we can say is that the correct solution must be between certain limits; we can say that rising prices are unjust to the creditor, and that prices which are falling more rapidly than the efficiency of production is increasing are certainly unjust to the debtor.

In trying to decide where, between these two limits, lies the correct policy which should be pursued there is one further point which is worth mentioning. The capitalist, who is arguing in favour of a falling price level, will probably suggest that any fall in the price of commodities is balanced by changes in people's ideas as to what is a reasonable standard of living and that the increased volume of goods is not really worth any more; in the language of the economist there is no increase in satisfaction. To this, however, the debtor may reply that a general increase in the efficiency of production does not necessarily involve an increase of efficiency in the case of particular industries or particular individuals; the borrower's efficiency may not have increased at all.

I cannot help feeling that there is a good deal of substance in this latter argument, and that consideration of the respective claims of debtor and creditor may well lead us to favour a policy of stable commodity prices.

FIXED RATES OF INTEREST

Apart from the question of debtor and creditor there is the closely allied question of capital which is entitled to a fixed rate of interest, the fixed charges as they are often called.

Here the interests of the community are clear. What the investor asks for is security, and if he gets, in addition to security of capital, the assurance that prices will not be raised he has received as much as he can reasonably expect. There is no reason why he should be given an additional premium in the shape of falling prices.

THE DISTRIBUTION OF WEALTH

The distribution of wealth among various classes in the community is a matter which the author has discussed elsewhere (4), and it is only necessary to refer to certain well-known results with which we are immediately concerned.

The increased efficiency of production which results from greater knowledge and the use of improved methods of manufacture creates additional wealth, and the price level is one of the factors which determines how this additional wealth is to be distributed.

If commodity prices are falling and wages remain fixed, then it is clear that the wage-earner will secure a proportional share in the improved output and that the owner of bonds or shares carrying a fixed rate of interest will do the same. There will be no change in the distribution of wealth.

Alternatively, if prices and wages both remain unchanged, the wage-earner will derive no benefit from the increased efficiency of production. It follows that a stable price level should be associated with a rising scale of wages, the rate of increase being not less than the rate of increase in the efficiency of production, an increase which may be assumed, for the sake of argument, to be 2 per cent. per annum. The expression "not less than the rate of increase in the efficiency of production" is used advisedly, for it is possible to argue that wages should be increased at a somewhat greater rate than this in order to secure, in the course of time, a more uniform distribution of wealth. We shall return to this matter in Chapter VIII.

There is one further point. If prices are made

stable instead of being allowed to fall, the bond-holder derives no benefit from the increasing efficiency of production, and the whole increase in the volume of production becomes available for the wage-earner. In other words, the stabilisation of prices should enable wages to be raised at a higher rate than the rate of increase in the efficiency of production. In fact it becomes possible, not only to increase the total volume of production, but also to increase the proportion of that production which is allotted to the wage-earner.

PRICES AND PROFITS

A rising price level enables the trader to sell his goods at a larger profit than he was entitled to assume when he bought them, and a belief that prices will continue to rise is therefore a stimulus to trade. To a lesser degree rising prices also stimulate industry, for the manufacturer purchases his materials in a lower market and sells his output in a higher one. Now expanding trade tends to cause rising prices and we thus discover a chain of cause and effect which tends to create instability; booms tend to be larger and slumps deeper than would otherwise be the case.

This well-known and much discussed effect has led many writers to advocate policies which have for their object the stabilisation of prices. Other economists have argued that fluctuations in trade are desirable because they stimulate progress, but the argument need not I think be taken very seriously.

Slumps always involve a great deal of unemployment and distress, and the ideal system would obviously secure the necessary rate of progress without the assistance of these painful disturbances. We may therefore accept the view that fluctuations in the activity of trade should be reduced as far as possible, and that the stabilisation of prices is a policy which would contribute to the attainment of that ideal.

Now the trader's desire to secure a profit is a short period affair, and the industrialist's influence in the same direction may be regarded as belonging to the medium period, and the magnitude of the changes which occur in the price level over short and medium periods of time are evidently of sufficient magnitude to influence both the policies of traders and industrialists and also their actual profits. It is reasonable to argue therefore that a greater degree of stability in the price level would tend to minimise the intensity of booms and depressions.

Passing now to the question of the long period trend of prices we find that the matter is somewhat controversial. There are some writers who have taken the argument which has been applied above to short and medium period effects, and have applied it to the long period also. They have thus reached the conclusion that, while a policy of rapidly falling prices would be objectionable and would depress trade, a policy aimed at stabilising prices would be unduly stimulating and would tend to intensify the fluctuations which it is one of our chief desires to prevent. A policy of stable incomes is therefore advocated, with the idea that such a policy would tend to minimise the intensity of industrial fluctuations, but the argument appears to involve an assumption which is not necessarily true in practice.

At a time when the efficiency of production is increasing a policy of stabilising incomes is presumably the same thing, at least in the long run, as a policy of allowing commodity prices to fall at the same rate as that at which efficiency is increasing, a rate which we have assumed to be about 2 per cent. per annum.

In examining this proposal it must be remembered, however, that we are now dealing with changes in the price level of smaller amount than those which are involved in the short and medium period effects, and that we are no longer entitled to assume that selling prices are advancing more rapidly than costs. If we assume, and we are surely entitled to make this assumption, that the monetary and economic system of the future is to be a definite improvement on the system of the past, then we are entitled to assert that wages will be raised at such a rate that there will be no excessive profits and that currency and credit will be allowed to expand in such a way that there is no artificial and unnecessary restriction in the supply of these necessary ingredients in the scheme of industrial prosperity.

In dealing with the long period trend of prices

the relationship between prices, profits and the activity of trade must not therefore be taken too seriously, since there are other factors which are of at least equal importance which must be taken into consideration in attempting to forecast the course of events. In particular, allowance must be made for changes in rates of wages and account must be taken of the influence which may be exerted by monetary policy. If these other factors are dealt with on a reasonable basis there appears to be no valid reason why a policy directed towards the stabilisation of prices should occasion any undue measure of instability in the economic structure as a whole.

SUMMARY OF THE ARGUMENT

We have now examined the effect of changing prices on the relationship between debtor and creditor, their influence on the distribution of wealth between different classes in the community, and their effect on the profits of trade and industry.

In each case we have reached the conclusion that the balance of advantages lies in the direction of stable prices, and it will be our business to examine, in future chapters, how far this ideal can be realised.

At the same time we have noted that stable prices should be associated with rising wages, the rate of increase being not less than the rate of increase in the efficiency of production. (5)

THE ORTHODOX POSITION

The orthodox economist would no doubt accept the statements made above regarding the disadvantages of an unstable price level, but there is another aspect of the matter which, in orthodox doctrine, outweighs in importance all such considerations.

In the monetary system of the nineteenth century there existed no instrument of management for the special control of the trade balance, and the necessary adjustment between imports and exports was made to depend on changes in the price level brought about by the ebb and flow of gold. Now for the effective working of this mechanism it is necessary that wages and commodity prices should be flexible, and the efficient working of the system is therefore incompatible with the stabilisation of prices. The supporter of the fixed gold standard cannot consistently become a supporter of the policy of stabilising prices.

It is at this point that the author is compelled to part company with the orthodox economist who advocates a return to the fixed gold standard with all that it implies.

The author holds that the monetary system of the nineteenth century is obsolete, that it involves unstable prices and much unnecessary restriction of credit, and he believes that a new and better system can be devised which will obviate both these disadvantages. It is one of the characteristics of this new system that it makes it possible for us to accept whole-heartedly and without reservation the ideal of a stable price level, leaving us free to discuss how far our ideal is attainable and what instruments are available for its realisation.

CHAPTER V

INFLATION AND DEFLATION

THE MEANING OF THE TERMS

THE dictionary meaning of the word inflation is "an undue expansion or increase," and in this general sense the word may evidently be applied to almost anything.

In discussions on monetary theory, the words inflation and deflation are often used, but the meaning attached to them is not uniform and is often not clearly defined. They seem to have been originally applied to the currency and to have been employed in the dictionary meaning of an undesirable increase or decrease in the volume of money, and they are still used in that sense. The difficulty has arisen, however, that the question of what is and what is not a desirable increase in the volume of money is largely a matter of opinion. Some writers have therefore used the words to mean an expansion or contraction of the currency whether desirable or not.

Other writers have applied the words to the price level, or to currency changes which have led to rising or falling prices. Yet other writers have made use of the expression "profit inflation," which of course is quite legitimate if the words are used in a dictionary and not in a technical sense.

Again, in popular discussions on the monetary problem, the words inflation and deflation have come to possess a special and rather sinister meaning. Inflation is associated with a large expansion of the currency, a general loss of confidence and a continuous rise in prices, such as occurred in Germany shortly after the Great War. Deflation, on the other hand, is associated with trade depression and severe unemployment, such as occurred in Great Britain between 1920 and 1931.

Finally, we have the adjectives "inflationary" and "deflationary" employed without any indication as to whether they apply to the currency or the price level or profits or something else, and the confusion of thought is complete.

Now it is of course true that an expansion of the currency, a rise of prices and abnormal profits may occur simultaneously and that these effects may be closely connected with one another, but it is nevertheless clear that the connection between the three factors is not sufficiently close for us to regard them as different aspects of a single variable, and it is necessary that inflation and deflation should be more precisely defined.

So far as the present essay is concerned the word inflation will be given a special technical meaning and will be applied to any condition of affairs in which prices are rising, and the word deflation will be used in relation to falling prices, but before attempting an exact definition it is necessary to direct our attention to another important point which must also be taken into consideration.

Reference has already been made to the fact that changes in the volume of currency may be associated with rising or falling prices, but the volume of currency is not the only factor which influences the price level; there are in fact a variety of factors to be considered. It may therefore happen that the effect of one factor which, acting alone, would produce a rising price level may be neutralised by the effect of another factor which, acting alone, would produce a falling price level, and it is necessary to decide how we are to deal with a situation in which a factor which is obviously inflationary fails to produce inflation.

An almost identical problem arises in mechanics in connection with the definition of the word "force," and the mechanical analogy serves to suggest a solution to our problem.

We know that an object such as a piece of metal, which is left unsupported, falls to the ground, and we say that it is acted on by the force of gravity. On the other hand, if it is placed on a table it does not fall although the force of gravity is presumably still in existence.

The teacher of mechanics surmounts the difficulty by defining force as something which produces or *tends to produce* motion. This definition of force has caused some misgivings to those philosophers who make a special study of the foundations on which the theory of mechanics is erected, but the theory works well in practice and we need not concern ourselves with these philosophic doubts. Returning then to the problem of the weight and the table, we note that the situation is explained by saying that the force of gravity remains unchanged but that it is exactly neutralised by the upward pressure which is exerted on the piece of metal by the surface of the table.

Utilising this method of approach to our monetary problem we may now frame the following definitions:—

A rise in the general price level is described as inflation, and any factor is said to be inflationary if it produces or *tends to produce* a general rise in prices.

Similarly, a fall in the general price level is described as deflation, and any factor is said to be deflationary if it produces *or tends to produce* a fall in prices.

Having thus settled what is to be understood by the terms inflationary and deflationary, we are in a position to examine the effect of particular factors which influence or tend to influence the price level.

INERTIA

There are certain factors which influence prices and which in their turn are affected by changes in the price level in such a way that a trend once started tends to continue.

As particular factors come up for discussion in regard to their influence on prices, reference will also be made if necessary to the way in which the factor in question is in its turn affected by changes in the price level.

SUPPLY AND DEMAND

If spending increases while the supply of commodities remains unchanged prices tend to rise, so that increased spending is inflationary and reduced spending is deflationary.

On the other hand, an increased production of commodities while spending remains constant tends to depress prices, so that increased production is deflationary and reduced production is inflationary.

One of the difficulties which becomes apparent in the modern world from time to time is that the progress of invention may lead to over-production in particular industries. As soon as stocks begin to accumulate the price of the commodity concerned inevitably falls and the general price level is affected accordingly.

We may note in passing that schemes for stabilising the general price level cannot alleviate a situation of this sort, since monetary influences do not discriminate in favour of the particular industries which happen to be in difficulties. The only possible remedy is to reduce production, and the sooner this is effected, the less will be the general disturbance caused by the necessary readjustments.

WAGES

Wages enter into the cost of production and changes in wages tend to exert a corresponding influence on prices.

As regards the influence of prices on wages, the position is as follows:—

The rate of wages influences, to an important extent, the distribution of the national dividend among the various classes of the community, and is always the subject of keen discussion between employers and employed. Each side being unwilling to yield anything to the other, the general effect is that rates of wages possess a considerable measure of stability, and changes are unlikely to occur unless the pressure exerted exceeds a certain minimum.

Changes in the price level are of course of great importance to both employers and employed. Low prices turn the employer's profits into losses and he naturally presses for reductions in wages. High prices, on the other hand, reduce the amount of goods which the wage-earner can purchase for his wages, and he naturally tries to bring about an increase in wages so as to maintain the standard of living to which he is accustomed.

It is necessary therefore to recognise a kind of "quantum effect" in the relationship between the price level and wages. If the changes in the price level are small, wages will probably remain unaffected, whereas if important changes occur in the retail price level wages are likely to follow suit.

It will also be observed that changes in rates of wages are not brought about quickly, and that the pressure exerted by the price level on wages is not therefore a short period effect. It is an effect which occurs in the medium and long periods only.

Moreover, wages are an item of industrial costs, and higher wages therefore mean higher costs. Since higher costs mean higher prices and therefore higher wages, the effect tends to be cumulative.

A final point must be referred to and that is the relative bargaining power of employers and employed.

In the seventeenth and eighteenth centuries the bargaining power of the wage-earner was small, and economists formulated what was known as the iron law to the effect that the wage-earner's portion could never rise above what was necessary to maintain a bare existence. In the modern world matters are different. The wage-earner has nowadays considerable power both industrially and politically, and it must I think be assumed that, in the long run, his bargaining power is greater than that of the employer. It is at least true that the cumulative reactions between wages and the price level tend to contribute to the phenomenon of unlimited inflation, whereas unlimited deflation does not make its appearance.

THE TRADER

A successful business is expected to yield an adequate return on the capital invested in it, and it is expected to pay for the cost of management. If it yields more than this it has made a windfall profit, and every keen business man is on the lookout for opportunities for making such profits.

Now rising prices enable goods to be bought and sold again at a profit, and a belief that prices will continue to rise induces traders to hold rather larger stocks of commodities than they would otherwise, and the effect is to drive up prices still further. A rise in prices sets up reactions therefore which tend to cause a further rise, and a condition of rising prices must be regarded as in itself an inflationary influence.

As regards the time factor, the reaction of the trader to the state of the markets is practically instantaneous. Moreover, it is expensive and wasteful to keep goods which are not really wanted, and the holding of abnormal stocks of commodities is not likely to be kept up for long. It follows that the inflationary influence of rising prices is a short period effect so far as the trader is concerned.

THE MANUFACTURER

A manufacturer's decision as to whether he should expand or contract his business depends upon his views as to the future course of the markets. The immediate effect of a decision to increase production is that extra workmen are engaged, and the wages given to these men are spent on consumable commodities, so that such action is inflationary. There are, however, two distinct effects.

There is the instantaneous increase in the demand for commodities, which is inflationary and which, if of moderate amount, may be temporarily neutralised by the using up of existing stocks. Secondly, there is the increased production, which actually reaches the market after a certain lapse of time, and whose effect is deflationary.

If the new production is reallyneeded the deflationary tendency of the increased supply will be balanced by the inflationary tendency of the increased spending of the additional workers, and production will continue on the higher level without any permanent change in the price level.

On the other hand, if the manufacturer's prediction is incorrect, the only result of his efforts is to create a general disturbance in the market which will tend to discourage expansion both in his own industry and elsewhere. In that case the final deflationary influence of failure will more than counterbalance the temporary tendency towards inflation which occurs during the period of construction.

SAVING AND INVESTMENT

If a miser hoards his gold instead of spending it he thereby reduces the demand for commodities, and such action is deflationary. Furthermore, the withdrawal of the gold from circulation also tends, as we shall see in the next chapter, to depress prices and a further deflationary effect takes place.

In the modern world the hoarding of gold still goes on but it is much less common than it used to be. If a man has saved money it is more usual for him to try to add to his savings by investing the money so that it earns interest. Now investment means that money is spent on the construction of factories and for similar purposes and there is no withdrawal of money from circulation at all. The decreased demand for consumable goods is balanced by the increased demand for capital goods, and we may say that the deflationary tendency due to saving has been balanced by the inflationary tendency of investment.

This is not the whole story, however. When the factory has been completed extra workmen are engaged to operate it, and the situation is the same as that referred to in the previous section. In short, if new factories are successfully started, they will absorb workmen who are unemployed or who are being released by declining industries and they will increase the output of commodities without bringing any pressure to bear on the price level.

If the new enterprises are unsuccessful, however, the result is different. The ultimate effect is to discourage investment and to bring about a period of depression, and it is well to remember that it is the ultimate result rather than the temporary reactions which are of importance to the wage-earner and the investor.

THE ACTIVITY OF TRADE

The relationship between the price level and the activity of trade is an important matter which serves to bring out, not only the significance of the time factor, but also the complexity of many of the typical monetary problems with which we are called upon to deal. For the discussion of this particular problem it is necessary to anticipate two results which arise out of our discussion in the next chapter where we shall find that, over the short period, money is neutral so that considerations of supply and demand exercise a predominating influence, and secondly that, over the long period, a fixed or restricted quantity of money tends to depress prices when trade is active and tends to raise prices when trade is slack.

Now it has already been pointed out that, when trade is expanding, demand expands more quickly than supply so that prices tend to rise, and thus, over the short period, expanding trade is inflationary. Turning to the long period, however, and assuming that the quantity of money is fixed or is expanding less rapidly than the activity of trade, we find that expanding trade tends to lower prices and is therefore deflationary. That is to say, expanding trade is inflationary over the short period and may be deflationary over the long period.

This is not the place to introduce a discussion on the theory of the trade cycle, but, when we remember that rising prices in their turn tend to stimulate the activity of trade, it is easy to see that all the conditions are present which are usually associated with a state of instability.

PUBLIC CONFIDENCE

If a private individual believes that prices are going to rise he may buy a new suit a little earlier than he would have done otherwise, but such special purchases do not usually occur on a sufficiently large scale to be of serious importance. In normal times the attitude of the public towards the currency is one of neutrality tempered perhaps by a slight taint of latent suspicion.

There are two ways in which the natural complacency of the public may be upset and the latent suspicion may be fanned into activity. Doubts as to the reality of the assets may arouse suspicions as to the solvency of the banks, and depositors may try to withdraw their money and hoard currency. Doubts as to the financial policy of the government may arouse suspicions as to the stability of the currency, and people may try to get rid of their money and buy commodities.

A withdrawal of deposits tends to jeopardise the assets of the banks, and increases the very risks which the depositor desires to avoid. Similarly an abnormal demand for goods raises prices and still further depresses the value of the currency. Both effects tend therefore to be cumulative.

In both cases also the reactions are rapid and temporary. A bank must either take steps to restore the confidence of its depositors or it must close its doors and go out of business. If the currency is suspect, the government must either take steps to restore confidence in the currency or the currency will soon collapse altogether and become valueless.

Loss of confidence in the banks or in the currency are therefore short period effects of exceptional intensity.

CREDIT

In the preceding sections reference was made to the inflationary effect which is produced by the expansion of trade and industry. But in order that a desire to expand trade and industry may be translated into action money is necessary, and it does not always happen that the business man who is in a position to take effective action possesses the cash. It is at this point that the influence of the banks makes itself felt. The banks can lend the business man the money which he requires, and it is in this way that the banks can control or "manage" the monetary position.

At the same time it must be noted that the banks do not possess the power of increasing or decreasing credit at will. The granting of a loan is a transaction in which two people take part, and it is necessary that both parties should desire the granting of a credit before the loan can actually be made. At the outset therefore a desire on the part of the banks to restrict credit may be frustrated by the determination of the business community to pursue a policy of expansion and by their ability to obtain the money required in other ways, and a desire on the part of the banks to expand credit may be neutralised by the inability of eligible borrowers to frame appropriate schemes for expansion and their consequent reluctance to take any action. It is only when banks and business men are agreed upon a policy that inflationary or deflationary action is actually taken, and even then the action taken may be neutralised by any of the other factors which influence the course of prices.

AN UNBALANCED BUDGET

Normally a government balances its budget by collecting in taxation an amount equal to the amount of its expenditure. Under such circumstances a certain amount of purchasing power is withdrawn from the individual and is utilised by the government for purposes which are supposed to be of national importance, and the operation has no direct influence on the monetary situation.

It is by no means necessary, however, that the budget should be exactly balanced; in fact an exact balance is improbable, and it is necessary to consider the two alternative policies which are always available. One alternative is that the government may spend more than it receives and it may fill the gap either by printing notes or by borrowing: such a policy is obviously inflationary. The other alternative is that the government may collect more in taxes than it spends and may utilise the balance to pay off debt: such a policy is obviously deflationary. The collection of taxes is never a popular measure, however, and deflationary policies are never pushed to extremes. It is the alternative policy of inflation caused by an unbalanced budget which is of greater interest and importance.

As already stated, the gap between the receipts and expenditure of the government may be filled either by printing notes or by borrowing, and the question whether inflation will actually occur or not depends on the attitude of the public towards the currency notes and government securities. If private individuals are prepared to save their money instead of spending it, and take over and hoard the additional notes, and are prepared to subscribe to the government loans at normal rates of interest, the inflationary tendency of the unbalanced budget will be exactly neutralised by the deflationary activities of private individuals and neither inflation nor deflation will actually take place. It is clear therefore that the net result is largely determined by the attitude of the public.

Firstly, if the inflationary tendency of the budget is of moderate amount, and if public confidence is not disturbed, the inflationary tendency may be completely neutralised.

Secondly, if the excess expenditure of the government exceeds the saving capabilities of the public, and if the public retains its confidence in both the government and the currency, inflation is inevitable but takes place very slowly. This is what happened in most belligerent countries during the War.

Thirdly, if the public loses confidence in the solvency of the government, but retains its confidence in the currency, the inflation will be more rapid, but not so rapid that the government cannot retrieve the position if it makes a determined effort to do so.

Finally, if the public loses confidence in both the government and the currency, the inflation may well get beyond control and may lead to complete collapse.

A rapid rise in prices tends to cause government expenditure to increase more rapidly than the yield of taxation so that a rapid inflation gains impetus as it proceeds, and the difficulties of controlling it are correspondingly increased.

SUMMARY

The preceding section, which deals with the problem of the unbalanced budget, furnishes a convenient example which shows how the method of approach outlined in the opening sections of this chapter can be applied to the actual problems which we are called upon to discuss. The remaining sections of the chapter refer very briefly to other factors which influence the course of prices and which must enter into any discussion on the theory of money.

Two factors of fundamental importance have been intentionally omitted, that is to say, the influence of gold and the influence of foreign trade. These need more detailed examination and are dealt with elsewhere.

CHAPTER VI

THE QUANTITY OF MONEY

THE QUANTITY THEORY

IF a given number of transactions have to be settled, payment can be made equally well in gold valued at 100 shillings an ounce or in silver valued at 2 shillings an ounce. The only difference is that the weight of silver required to settle a given debt is fifty times as great as the corresponding weight of gold, and, except for the inconvenience of transporting the larger weight of silver, either currency serves the purpose equally well. Now the weight of gold or silver required to pay for a unit quantity of any commodity is what we call the price, and we are thus led to the first fundamental principle in the theory of money: the quantity of money required to settle a given transaction is the quantity of goods or services multiplied by the price. More generally the total quantity of money required to settle a number of transactions is the sum total of the money values of the individual transactions, and the money value of each transaction is the volume of commodities multiplied by the price.

For the purpose of discussion it is convenient to assume that the situation is represented by the transfer of a quantity of what may be called a generalised commodity which is sold at an average price or price level, but it is important to bear in mind that this method of expression is not exact and that the only correct form in which the principle can be expressed is that given in the previous paragraph. Failure to realise this has led to a great deal of rather futile discussion on the subject of Index Numbers.

Now money is of no value except for what it will buy, and people who receive money usually spend it again, so that the same money may change hands many times, and the average number of times which money changes hands in the course of a year (or other unit of time) is known as the velocity of circulation.

The second fundamental principle in the theory of money is that the total money value of the transactions settled in the course of a unit of time is equal to the quantity of money multiplied by the velocity of circulation.

These two principles may be combined into a common formula which may be stated as follows:—

The total value of business transactions per annum, which may be regarded as the volume of such transactions multiplied by the price level, is equal to the quantity of money in circulation multiplied by the velocity with which it circulates.

This is an identity, and on the face of things appears to be a proposition of great importance, but in actual fact the interpretation of the formula is a matter of considerable difficulty. Nevertheless the formula does possess an undoubted importance, and it is necessary to discuss both its significance and its limitations.

An equation such as that set forth above may be regarded from two distinct points of view.

From the statistical point of view it enables us to deduce one factor in the equation if the other factors are known. Considerable use is in fact made of the equation for this purpose.

From the economic point of view the equation is, however, of much greater significance. It is in effect an economic law which enables us to infer that certain causes will lead to certain results, and the question then arises as to whether it is true, or alternatively, if it is not absolutely true, whether it is true in certain circumstances and with certain limitations.

Perhaps the nature of the problem with which we have to deal may be made clearer by means of an anology.

SIGNIFICANCE OF THE EQUATION

The volume of liquid in a cylindrical vessel is equal to the area of the cross-section multiplied by the depth of the liquid. The equation involves three quantities, and, if two are independently determined, the value of the third is dependent on the known values of the other two. Thus, if a certain measure of beer is poured into a pint pot of known cross-section the depth of the liquid is *dependent* on the other two quantities.

Now most of the factors which enter into our discussion of economic problems are known to exhibit a certain amount of resistance to change. This resistance may resemble mechanical inertia and may be a resistance to the rapidity of the change, or it may resemble the elastic reaction of a spring which resists all change irrespective of the speed at which the change takes place.

In searching for an interpretation of our equation it is therefore profitable to consider the relative amounts of inertia and relative degrees of flexibility exhibited by each of the four quantities of which the equation is made up. If it can be shown that one particular factor exhibits less inertia and is more flexible than the other three, then we are entitled to say that this is the quantity which is *dependent* on the values of the others.

A SIMPLE METALLIC CURRENCY

Before the development of the banking system, when gold and silver and other objects of real value were the only forms of money, the whole position was very much simpler, and the interpretation of the quantity equation in such cases was very much easier than it is to-day. It will help to clarify our ideas if we open our discussion by considering the application of our equation to these more elementary conditions.

We begin by noting that, in the absence of credit

facilities, all transactions had to be dealt with on a cash basis. The merchant requiring goods for his trade or the manufacturer needing raw materials for his workshop had to be prepared to produce the money to pay for them. If the money was not available trade and industry must alike be suspended and, if the quantity of money available was limited, the volume of business or the price level or both had to adjust themselves to the amount of money actually available.

As is well known, the various factors which enter into our equation are subject to short period fluctuations, but a discussion of these matters may conveniently be postponed, and we may fix our attention on what may be called long period effects.

A further simplification may also be introduced into our argument. If we consider what is meant by the velocity of circulation, we must I think reach the conclusion that it depends upon habits and customs which are not likely to undergo rapid change; in fact we may go further and say that (apart from temporary fluctuations) changes in the velocity of circulation are likely to be very slow indeed, and that we shall not be involved in any serious error if we regard the velocity of circulation as a constant.

Now we know that there were often particular epochs when the quantity of gold and silver in active circulation did not change to any great extent. Let us therefore apply our equation to this particular case and see what deductions may be drawn from it.

The quantity of money and the velocity of circulation being constant, our equation tells us that the volume of business transactions is inversely proportional to the price level, so that expanding business involves falling prices and *vice versa*. But we know that falling prices reduce profits and depress trade, so that any tendency towards increased business activity is nipped in the bud by a falling price level. We must conclude therefore that a fixed quantity of money is a definite hindrance to progress; expanding business needs an increasing quantity of money in order to avoid the reactionary effect of falling prices.

Let us now vary our assumptions. Let us suppose that new sources of gold and silver are discovered so that the volume of money expands. Our equation now tells us that, if the expansion of business lags behind the expansion of the quantity of money, prices will rise. But we know that rising prices stimulate trade and enterprise, and we therefore conclude that an influx of gold and silver is likely to herald a period of progress and expanding trade.

Now there is historical evidence which seems to show that events did actually follow the course which is suggested by our equation (6), and we are therefore justified in saying that our argument appears to contain a certain measure of truth.

PAPER MONEY

At a certain stage in the financial development of the world it was discovered that a promise to pay, if given by a reliable individual or body of individuals, is just as valuable as the money itself, and thus paper money came into existence.

Now paper money is easily printed and the invention of paper money disposed for ever of the difficulty that progress might be hampered by lack of money, but it did not solve the currency problem, for the newly invented paper money gave rise to problems of its own. Experience very soon showed that just as much trouble might be created by having too much money as by having too little. If the quantity of money is allowed to expand too rapidly, the volume of legitimate business is unable to keep pace with it, and our quantity equation tells us that prices will rise. The result is that trade is unduly stimulated, the excessive stimulus leads to the production of particular goods which nobody wants, and the result is chaos and collapse.

It has therefore been found necessary to take steps to regulate the quantity of money so that it expands neither too slowly nor too quickly, and we are thus introduced to the modern problem of the management of money, a problem which is very closely related to the problem of the price level which it is our purpose to discuss in the present essay.

For the moment, the point which it is necessary

to emphasise is that the management of money is essential to the working of the modern economic machine. Furthermore, the better the management the better and the more smoothly will the machine be found to work.

THREE MONETARY CIRCULATIONS

The modern monetary system differs in various ways from the elementary monetary system which has been discussed in the preceding sections. For one thing, the time factor is of fundamental importance and cannot be neglected in any detailed discussion of the subject. But this is not the only complication. In the modern economic system there are at least three distinct monetary circulations which exhibit different characteristics and which must be dealt with separately. These three circulations are: the circulation of cash, the circulation of bank money and the circulation of credit.

It will be necessary for us to examine each of these circulations in turn, and we must consider whether each circulation influences the price level and if so in what way, but the first matter which naturally arises out of our method of treatment is the question how far the three circulations can be regarded as independent.

The accepted business practice is that a debt can be settled either in cash or by cheque, and from what may be called the business point of view bank money is therefore equivalent to cash. In actual fact, however, there are certain transactions which are normally settled in cash and others which are normally settled by cheque, and we can say as a matter of common observation that custom in such matters changes only very gradually. There is undoubtedly a tendency for transactions settled by cheque to increase and for transactions settled in cash to diminish, but the process is so slow that it is unlikely to produce results of significant amount even over a period of, say, a decade. For shorter periods the method of making payment for any particular type of transaction may be regarded as fixed. In other words, the circulation of cash and the circulation of bank money may be regarded as independent unless we are dealing with very long periods of time.

The distinction between cash and bank money on the one hand and credit on the other is more definite and hardly needs detailed examination.

When we come to the question of the relationship between the activity of trade and the volume of business dealt with by the various circulations we may note certain similarities and certain differences. Expanding trade is likely to cause an increase in the volume of business dealt with both by bank money and cash, but it is not likely to affect these two circulations in exactly the same proportion. Business of a speculative character is more likely to be settled by cheque, and expanding or contracting trade is likely to influence the bank circulation to a greater extent than the circulation of cash. However, for the moment we are more concerned with the similarities of these circulations than with their differences.

THE QUANTITY OF CASH

When a country makes use of a gold coinage and when gold is held by the central bank to the full amount of the notes issued, the total quantity of cash which is in circulation or which can be put into circulation is equal to the quantity of gold. In actual practice, however, there exist certain complications to which reference must be made before we come to examine the working of the cash circulation under the guidance of what we call the gold standard.

In 1844 Great Britain adopted the principle of the fiduciary issue, the system under which the Bank of England was authorised to issue notes backed by government securities up to a certain fixed amount in addition to such issues as were made in virtue of the Bank's holding of gold. The amount of the fiduciary issue remained unchanged until the abandonment of the gold standard during the Great War. Under the conditions which actually existed the working of the system was precisely the same as if an equivalent amount of gold had actually existed in the vaults of the Bank, and it is clear that the working of the monetary circulation can be dealt with exactly as if the phantom gold representing the fiduciary issue possessed a real existence.

Other countries adopted the principle of issuing notes backed by a certain percentage of gold, but the number and importance of these countries was not sufficiently great to affect our problem to a material extent, and it is therefore convenient to ignore this particular complication also.

Certain important countries such as India and China retained a silver standard, but for the moment it is convenient to confine our attention to the working of the monetary system in those countries which adopted the gold standard, and to pass over the complications which arise from the existence of these two distinct standards.

Our main discussion starts therefore with the assumption that the gold standard was the accepted monetary system in the more important countries of the world during the latter half of the nineteenth century and the beginning of the twentieth, and that the quantity of cash in each of these countries was determined by the volume of gold circulating as coinage or held by the central banks.

This quantity of gold in any particular country might be increased or diminished by transfers of gold from or to other countries, and the total quantity of gold in all the gold standard countries might be increased by the production of new gold by the mines, but we note that these movements are not rapid. A flow of gold from one country to another of sufficient magnitude to cause appreciable reactions is a matter of years, while the influence of gold production on the monetary gold of the world must be regarded as a matter of decades.

THE ACTIVE CIRCULATION

We make the assumption then that the total quantity of cash in the country depends upon the quantity of gold in the coinage or held by the central bank, but not all this money is in active circulation. A part is probably held in reserve by the central bank, a part is held by member banks, and only the balance is held by the public.

Again, the individual may not employ the whole of his money in the same way. In extreme cases he may hoard some of his money in a stocking, and even in more normal cases he may not limit himself to the exact amount of money which is necessary to cover his anticipated purchases up to the date on which he is entitled to his next payment of wages or salary. He probably allows a little extra to provide for contingencies.

This means to say that even the money in the hands of the public is not all in active circulation, there is a certain amount which must be regarded as a reserve.

Now it is clear that money which is lying in the vaults of a central bank can have no direct effect on the actions of individuals, and that our quantity equation must be held to apply, not to the total volume of money, but to the volume of money in active circulation.

It is also clear that a call for additional money arising out of the needs of expanding business will be largely met by putting into circulation the reserves of cash which are held either by the banks or by individuals. In other words, the volume of active money is elastic, and, within limits, changes in the active circulation may be brought about without calling forth any reaction either on the part of individuals or the banks.

When we come to large changes in the circulation, the matter is different. The amount of cash actually in existence evidently fixes an upper limit to the total volume of the circulation, and a less definite limit is set in the other direction by the policy of the banks. Cash does not earn any interest, and an excess of cash stimulates the banks to expand credit with a view to getting the cash into circulation again.

A clear distinction must therefore be drawn between large changes in the volume of money and small ones. For small changes the volume of money in active circulation may be regarded as elastic and ready to adjust itself to the varying needs of business, but for large changes approaching the limits to which we have referred the volume of money becomes less elastic, and increasing resistance is developed as these limits are approached.

THE VELOCITY OF CIRCULATION

Reference must now be made to the fact that our quantity equation can be used in two distinct ways, and that in consequence the expression "velocity of circulation" may have two distinct meanings.

We may on the one hand regard the total quantity of cash in existence as the quantity of money to which our equation is to be applied, and this method has the advantage that in practice the total quantity of cash in existence is known with considerable accuracy, whereas the quantity of money in active circulation can only be guessed at. If our equation is used in this way the velocity of circulation may conveniently be described as the *apparent* velocity.

On the other hand, we may regard the quantity of money in active circulation as the quantity to which our equation is to be applied, and this procedure has important advantages for the purpose of purely theoretical discussion. Over moderate periods of time it enables us to treat the velocity of circulation as a constant, and the number of variables in our equation is reduced thereby from four to three, and this greatly simplifies our argument. If our equation is used in this way the velocity of circulation may be called the *real* velocity.

In our subsequent discussion it will be assumed therefore that changes in the apparent velocity of circulation are in fact caused by changes in the quantity of money which is taking part in the active circulation, and that the real velocity of circulation is only subject to very gradual changes, at least under normal conditions. It is no doubt true that, in times of rapid inflation, the velocity of circulation is temporarily increased, but such a condition of affairs must be definitely regarded as abnormal.

NEUTRAL MONEY

Recent controversies about inflationary and deflationary policies have introduced the idea of neutral money. Since inflationary and deflationary policies are both regarded as objectionable, it is argued that the correct policy is that money should be "neutral."

Without prejudicing our discussion by expressing any opinion as to the merits or practicability of the suggested policy, we may, I think, welcome the addition of the word "neutral" to our vocabulary of economic terms, and we may say:—

A factor in the monetary situation is regarded as *neutral* when it is neither inflationary nor deflationary, that is to say when it does not exert any appreciable influence on the trend of prices.

Now it has already been pointed out that every firm or individual, consciously or unconsciously, keeps a stock of money or a deposit at the bank in order to meet certain definite and distinct requirements. A certain sum of money is required, for example, to balance weekly or monthly variations between expenditure and receipts, a further sum of money may be held to provide for unforeseen contingencies, and a still further sum may represent money which has been saved and which is awaiting a suitable opportunity for investment; and it is of course clear that only the money which is required for the first of these objects is really kept in circulation at all. The other money does not become involved in the general circulation or at least it circulates very much more slowly.

Now the need for money to provide for additional payments is most readily met by utilising the money which the firm or individual already holds, and the necessary money simply passes into circulation therefore without any fuss or without any attention being drawn to what is really happening. Nor does the adjustment involve any delay.

The effect of such practices is to make the volume of money in active circulation elastic, or making use of the phrase which appears at the head of this section we may say:—

Under normal conditions and for small fluctuations money is always neutral.

It is a well-known fact that the effect of monetary management is exerted spasmodically, and that it is mainly in evidence either at the height of a boom or at the depth of a slump, and the above proposition explains why this must be so. Monetary pressure of small or moderate amount simply calls into circulation money which has been lying idle, or drives it out of circulation, as the case may be.

Moreover, this flexibility in the supply of money is based on the deeply rooted habits of individuals and is not in a general way amenable to the influence of either banks or governments.

THE SIGNIFICANCE OF THE CASH CIRCULATION

Under modern conditions the circulation of bank money is perhaps nine or ten times the circulation of cash, and it is quite clear that the circulation of cash cannot exert on the activity of trade the direct pressure which it would do in the simple monetary system which we have previously discussed.

One fact of fundamental importance has already been alluded to: there are certain types of transaction which are always settled in cash and not by cheque, and it is therefore possible to deal with the circulation of bank money and the circulation of cash as separate entities, each providing certain necessary facilities which are distinct from, but expand and contract in sympathy with, the activity of business as a whole. We are entitled therefore to treat the cash circulation as a separate problem and to discuss the reactions which arise when the quantity of cash is in excess or defect of the requirements of the moment.

For well-known reasons an excess or a deficiency of cash is able to influence the policy of the banks, and it is through the action of the central bank that the circulation of cash may ultimately exert an influence on the activity of trade. But the cash position is not the only factor which influences the policy of the central bank, and it is therefore clear that such influence as it is able to exert can only make itself apparent after a considerable period of time. If action by the central bank may take a year or two to influence the activity of trade, the influence of the cash position must be even less rapid.

The relationship between the quantity of cash and the price level may therefore be summarised as follows:—

Over short periods the volume of money in active circulation is free to expand and money is neutral. The tendency for prices to rise or fall in sympathy with expanding or contracting trade is not subject to resistance, and this factor causes prices to move in the opposite direction to that which our quantity equation might lead us to expect.

Over medium periods the quantity of cash in the country may exert an influence on the policy of the central bank in the sense that a fixed quantity of cash is deflationary when the activity of trade is abnormally high and inflationary when trade is abnormally depressed.

Over the long period the quantity of cash, acting through its influence on the policy of the central bank, is one of the factors which influences the price level, and it does so in the sense which our quantity equation would lead us to expect. A certain quantity of cash is necessary to finance any given volume of business transactions at any given velocity: if the actual quantity of cash is in excess of this ideal quantity, prices will rise; if there is a deficiency, prices will fall.

BANK MONEY

Business which is settled by cheque leaves a definite record of each individual transaction, and it is therefore possible to study the circulation of bank money in a manner which is not possible with the circulation of cash. Information is available as to the total volume of deposits and as to the amount of money dealt with by the clearing houses, and this information (so far as it is made public) enables the apparent velocity of circulation to be calculated, and the results thus obtained provide a useful indication of the activity of trade.

The practice of allowing interest on deposits which are subject to notice of withdrawal also gives a certain amount of information as to the amount of money which is being "hoarded," as opposed to the amount which is in active circulation, although one is not entitled to claim that deductions of this nature can be made with great accuracy.

At this point in our argument it is perhaps desirable to emphasise the distinction between credit, which involves tying up money for a certain period of time, and money itself, which is simply a medium for facilitating the exchange of commodities and services, and the reader must be reminded that we are now considering the banking business in its purely monetary aspect.

If then we observe, as we do in fact observe, that depositors only find it necessary to keep a part of their deposits on "current account" we are entitled to draw the inference that the quantity of bank money in existence, that is to say the total value of the deposits, is always in excess of the monetary needs of the community.

Moreover, there is another fact which points to a similar conclusion. An increase in overdraft facilities would permit of a larger volume of business being dealt with for a given volume of deposits, and if there were any real demand for additional monetary facilities this practice would no doubt be adopted to a greater extent than is actually the case.

We conclude that, in the modern world, the quantity of bank money in existence at any particular moment is always more than sufficient to perform the monetary function of providing a medium of exchange, and lack of bank money (as distinct from lack of credit) never acts as a brake on the activity of trade and has therefore no influence on the price level. In other words, *bank money is always neutral.*

As applied to bank money therefore our quantity equation may be regarded as a convenient formula for determining any one of the four quantities of which it is composed when the other three are known, but it is nothing more. It does not disclose the existence of any force which is capable of influencing the course of events.

CREDIT

When goods are manufactured in one place and transported to another for distribution, or to form the raw material of some other industry, a certain amount of time is taken up in the period of transit, and the purchaser must either pay for the goods before he receives them or the seller must forgo payment, or the gap must be bridged by some intermediary. It is also necessary to hold stocks of goods, and these two groups of items, goods in stock and goods in transit, make up what is commonly called working capital, and the money involved in such transactions comes under the heading of what we have called credit.

Alongside the circulation of cash and the circulation of bank money already referred to we have therefore a circulation of credit which serves a somewhat similar purpose but which possesses characteristics of its own.

The first important thing to notice about credit, or rather about such credit as is used for financing working capital, is that the money required for additional working capital is normally obtained from the banks, so that an expansion or contraction of working capital usually involves a corresponding expansion or contraction of credit and *vice versa*.

This consideration explains the very close connection which exists between the volume of credit and the activity of trade, and it lies at the root of the discovery, which was made during the nineteenth century, that the management of credit is the most convenient and effective instrument at present known for the control of trade, and for checking the inherent tendency to uncontrolled inflation.

It is true that firms may be able to supply themselves with a certain amount of working capital without resorting to the banks. It is true that methods adopted by the banks for expanding or contracting credit are not always immediately effective; there may be a delay of months before the desired result actually ensues. It is also true that credit may be used for other purposes besides working capital such as stock exchange speculation or disguised investment.

Nevertheless, in spite of all reservations and limitations, no better system of management than that based on the control of the volume of credit has hitherto been devised.

Another very important thing to notice is that the velocity with which credit circulates is actually determined by the velocity of circulation of the commodities on which the credit is secured, and that it differs in this respect from the circulation of cash and the circulation of bank money. If production and consumption are well balanced, the velocity of circulation is high, whereas the production of unwanted goods upsets the even flow of credit and reduces the velocity.

In the last phase of a boom one of the conspicuous features is an urgent demand for additional credit to finance this unwanted accumulation of working capital. As soon as credit is restricted the bubble bursts, trade declines and prices collapse.

SUMMARY

(i) In discussing the application of the quantity theory of money to modern conditions, attention has been drawn to the fact that there are three distinct circulations to be considered—the circulation of cash, the circulation of bank money and the circulation of credit.

(ii) For short periods the volume of money taking part in the active circulation is elastic and therefore under normal conditions and for small fluctuations money is neutral.

(iii) The circulation of cash is much smaller than the circulation of either bank money or credit, and, under normal conditions, the volume of cash has no *direct* influence on the price level. The volume of cash does, however, affect the policy of the banks, and may therefore affect the price level indirectly. The action is somewhat sluggish and must be regarded as a medium and long period effect. In the past the volume of cash has probably been the principal factor in determining the long period trend of prices.

(iv) The volume of bank money is elastic and has no influence on the price level, that is to say, bank money is always neutral.

(v) For the credit circulation the velocity is determined by the movement of goods and not by the factors which normally influence the movement of money.

(vi) The volume of credit is closely linked with the amount of working capital employed in trade, and the power of controlling the volume of credit can be made use of to control the activity of trade. Changes in the activity of trade may in turn affect the price level, but the process is slow and uncertain.

CHAPTER VII

GOLD

THE STERLING STANDARD

THE gold standard of the nineteenth century—the sterling standard as it has not inaptly been called (7)—represented an important but none the less temporary stage in the evolution of monetary systems. It represented a period of transition from the unmanaged metallic currencies of the past to the managed paper currencies of the future. Its success showed that currency management is an art which can exercise an important and beneficial influence on the course of trade, while its recent collapse has shown that the system in its nineteenth-century form is no longer adequate to cope with modern conditions.

The essential characteristic of that system was the use of credit control as an instrument of management, and it is interesting to note that this single instrument was sufficient to maintain a fair degree of stability in the monetary system of the world for nearly a century.

The successful working of the system depended in practice not only on the deliberate management of the Bank of England, but also on the operation of two factors which are sometimes referred to as "automatic" controls.

The first of these controls had reference to the trade balance. It has often been described and has been referred to by the author elsewhere. (8)

The second of these controls had reference to the price level and arises simply from the fact that a rise in the value of gold stimulates the production of the precious metal. A fall in the general price level of commodities is equivalent to a rise in the value of gold, and in due course the increased production of gold raises the gold stocks of the central banks and tends to check the fall in prices. The process must evidently be very slow, but price movements during the nineteenth century seem to suggest that it was actually of considerable importance.

We see therefore that the monetary system of the nineteenth century involved the existence of these two "automatic" controls in addition to the control which was deliberately exercised by the management of credit. It was almost as if some kindly providence had provided mankind with the necessary guidance during the period of its economic childhood, and had furnished the world with an economic system which was able to yield reasonably good results with only a very moderate degree of intelligent control.

The satisfactory working of the system depended in fact on the existence of certain favourable conditions of which the most important were:—

(i) Great Britain was the only important creditor

nation, and she therefore possessed the power to make her management effective. The other creditor nations which made their appearance towards the end of the period were not sufficiently powerful to upset the working of the system.

(ii) Great Britain was willing to lend her money abroad.

(iii) Great Britain had already acquired considerable experience of foreign investment and was able to arrange that the money lent should be profitably invested.

(iv) There was a reasonable balance between the volume of suitable investments and the volume of savings which was necessary to finance them. The question is a controversial one, but I suggest that the existence of this balance is not inherent in the system and that it must either be attributed to the business foresight of the British investor or else it must be regarded as a fortunate coincidence.

(v) Great Britain adopted a policy of free trade, and this lent to the system a degree of flexibility which it would not otherwise have possessed.

(vi) Great Britain held a unique position as a pioneer of modern industrial methods, and it may reasonably be argued that it was this special circumstance that rendered free trade possible.

(vii) There was a reasonable balance between the quantity of gold required for the working of the system and the amount which was actually available. A necessary factor in securing this balance was the absence of serious hoarding. Apart from this it must I think be regarded as a fortunate coincidence.

(viii) The smooth working of the system required that prices in general and wages in particular should be flexible, and prices and wages were in fact sufficiently flexible for the purpose.

The situation which exists in the world to-day is fundamentally different from that which existed during the nineteenth century. There are now at least three important creditor countries instead of one, and, moreover, the economic problems which these countries have to solve are not identical, and it is necessary to accept the fact that the policies adopted are different now and are always likely to remain so.

The two new creditor countries—France and the United States—have both tried to pursue a policy of foreign investment and have both failed to make that policy effective. Both these countries are committed to policies of protection, and the adoption of a policy of world-wide free trade is quite beyond the scope of practical politics, even if it could be shown that such a policy is desirable. Again, for various reasons, wages in the modern world have become less flexible than formerly and the prices of certain goods and services (transport, for example) have followed suit.

It seems to be impossible to avoid the conclusion that the monetary system of the nineteenth century is not workable under modern conditions and that it cannot be made so. If an attempt is made to restore international trade on the basis of a fixed gold standard, only one result is possible—there will be a temporary burst of prosperity followed by another collapse.

GOLD IN THE FUTURE

The employment of a gold coinage and the use of gold in connection with international trade were essential features in the monetary system of the nineteenth century. Gold was in fact expected to exercise the following distinct functions:—

(i) To provide a national currency in the form of a gold coinage. So far as this function is concerned, however, modern experience has shown that notes can be made to serve exactly the same purpose as a gold coinage, and they are if anything more convenient to handle. Gold is not therefore necessary for this purpose.

(ii) To act as a backing for the note issue, and thus prevent inflation by providing a check on the number of notes issued. On this point recent experience shows that the supposed check is, under modern conditions at least, neither effective nor desirable. It is not effective because in times of real emergency it is always thrown overboard. It is not desirable because it does not act in the right way. If trade and industry are expanding on sound and legitimate lines, and additional money is necessary in order to meet normal business requirements, that additional money should be provided independently of whether the country can increase its supply of gold or not.

(iii) To act as a basis of credit. For reasons which it is unnecessary to go into here, it is the accepted banking practice to maintain, as nearly as possible, a fixed ratio between the volume of cash and the volume of credit. If the quantity of cash is made to depend on the quantity of gold, a relationship is thus established between the quantity of gold and the volume of credit.

Here again the writer must submit that the check is neither effective nor desirable. It is not effective because the government has always the power to alter the basis of the structure by increasing or diminishing the note issue, or alternatively it can produce similar results by unbalancing its budget. It is not desirable because the volume of credit should depend on the state of trade and not on the supply of gold. The writer's contention is that signs of over-trading provide adequate justification for the restriction of credit, but that restriction of credit should never be used under any other circumstances. This proposition is elaborated elsewhere in the present essay.

(iv) To play its part in the control of the trade balance.

In regard to this function the author has endeavoured to show elsewhere, as already explained in the opening chapter of this essay, that the gold standard provides a very unsatisfactory mechanism for the control of the trade balance, and that the correct instrument of management for this purpose is a system of variable exchanges. The proposed system can be worked in conjunction with a gold standard, but it can also be worked equally well without it.

(v) To regulate the long period trend of world prices.

This question of the price level is the central topic of discussion in the present essay, and the author has endeavoured to show that gold provides a very unsatisfactory standard of value, and that a better regulation of the price level can be secured by other methods.

(vi) To perform the functions of an international currency.

There is some difference between the functions which are performed by national and international currencies respectively. In the former case the currency is actually the means of payment, whereas in the latter case the means of payment is a bank draft or a bill of exchange, and the international currency is only required to deal with the balance which remains when the flow in one direction does not balance the flow in the other.

To a large extent the outstanding balance is normally made up by means of loans and investments, but this method of balancing the international account is liable to fail in a crisis, and there appears to exist therefore a real demand for some form of international currency which is free from the risk of sudden failure. As a result of long-established custom and tradition, gold and silver do appear to inspire a degree of confidence which cannot be secured by any other means, and it would appear that they provide a form of international currency for which there is no effective substitute.

Summing up our attempted forecast of the monetary system of the future, it may be said that cheques, currency notes and token coins appear to provide all the facilities which are demanded of a national currency, and there does not appear to be any adequate reason why the use of gold and silver for such purposes should be restored. Nor does there appear to be any adequate reason for burying in the vaults of a central bank a quantity of gold and silver which is supposed to represent on some purely artificial scale an arbitrary proportion of the notes which have been issued. (9)

On the other hand, there is reason to believe that gold and silver will continue to play a useful part in international monetary affairs, but it will be a subordinate part, and especially so if a comparison is made between the new position which they will occupy in the future and the almost fanatical worship which has been accorded to them in the past.

THE PRICE OF GOLD

Perhaps the greatest difference between the monetary theory of the future and the monetary theory of the past will be found in our attitude towards gold and silver as standards of value. In the nineteenth century gold was regarded as a standard of value, and it was the custom to discuss the problem of stabilising the price level of commodities. In the future we shall be able to make use of other methods for stabilising the price level, and we shall express ourselves differently: instead of saying that we wish to stabilise the price level of commodities, we shall say that we wish to stabilise the price of gold. The problem is essentially the same but we shall view it from a different angle. And having once oriented our minds to this new aspect of the matter, and thus obtained a clearer picture of the whole position, we shall find, I think, that the problem to be solved is less difficult than it appeared at first sight.

Recent events have gone to show that the price of gold is a very clumsy and unreliable standard to use for the control of the price level, and there is every reason to believe that better methods are available, and we are also entitled to assume that a reasonable measure of stabilisation is a practical possibility. Having thus secured such a measure of price stabilisation as the circumstances of the case permit, we can then deal with the price of gold on the same lines as those which we should adopt in dealing with any other commodity. It becomes simply a question of adjusting supply and demand.

The chief buyers—I will not say users—of gold are the central banks, and it is simply necessary for these institutions to act together and they can fix the price of gold at any figure they please. Of course there is always the difficulty of securing international co-operation, but this difficulty will be much reduced when it becomes possible to take a more reasonable and enlightened view of the whole problem.

HOARDING

There is a certain primitive instinct which impels people to hoard gold and silver in order to provide for future eventualities. If, over and above this, a rising price for the metal makes hoarding a profitable operation from the purely business point of view, then hoarding is likely to assume large and dangerous proportions. The abnormal demand which arises from the desire to add to existing hoards in turn drives up prices, and the process continues until by some means the vicious circle can be broken.

The behaviour of gold in this matter is somewhat paradoxical for it constitutes an exception to the otherwise universal rule that a rising price will cause a falling off in demand. In the early part of the present crisis gold behaved normally—the rising price arrested the flow of gold to India and caused some of the hoards there to be released, but in Europe in recent years the rising price has, for the reasons already given, encouraged hoarding and thereby increased the demand.

If hoarding is to be discouraged the price of gold must be prevented from rising, or at least the rise must be limited to a very low figure, certainly not more than 2 per cent. per annum.

Several governments have recently forbidden the private hoarding of gold, and it is of course possible to conceive of a monetary system in which gold is held entirely by the central banks and private hoarding is forbidden; it is also possible to conceive of a monetary system in which gold and silver play no part at all; but the world does not yet seem to be ripe for such developments. We must, I think, accept the fact that gold and silver will still play a part in monetary affairs for many years to come.

One thing is clear, however, the influence of gold will be purely mischievous unless the important gold-using countries of the world are prepared to co-operate in order to control the price. They must not only be prepared to refrain from acquiring gold for their central banks if the situation happens to demand such action, but they must be prepared if necessary to allow gold to flow out of the banks into private hoards. If such a policy is consistently pursued it is inconceivable that private hoarding can counteract the combined operations of the world's central banks.

INTERNATIONAL CO-OPERATION

International trade and international finance are essentially international problems which cannot be solved on a purely national basis, and a certain measure of international agreement is necessary for the successful operation of any international currency system whatever. The immediate problem of removing the existing monetary obstacles to international trade will be referred to in the next section, and here as elsewhere international co-operation is an essential condition of success. But, the reader will perhaps argue, international agreement on any question of importance is impossible under present conditions. Look at the Economic Conference of 1933, look at the various disarmament conferences, what is the good of talking about international agreement?

In reply to this argument I would venture to point out that we are discussing monetary policy and not disarmament. The great depression has made queer bed-fellows, and the lines of cleavage between the different groups are not political; they are purely accidental and fortuitous.

The international currency problem has special features in each particular country. Nevertheless it is not to any serious extent a national problem or a political problem: it is an intellectual problem. It is necessary for us to abandon a monetary theory adapted to the working of an obsolete monetary system which is no longer adequate to meet the needs of the present day, and it is necessary to develop a new and more elaborate monetary system based on a more general and more complete monetary theory. If those who are in a position to direct the monetary affairs of the world can be enabled to visualise the true character of the problem, it is unreasonable to suppose that agreement cannot be reached on what are after all merely matters of detail.

GOLD IN RELATION TO PRESENT PROBLEMS

The world has always been prone to an almost fanatical worship of gold and silver, and particularly so when gold is rising in value and when a profit can be realised by hoarding it. Moreover, there are several countries which have suffered recently from monetary inflation, and these countries are naturally imbued with a serious distrust of paper money. It is unlikely that those countries which are now on the gold standard will abandon it unless they are compelled to do so, and at the same time there are signs that those countries which have abandoned gold are anxious to return to it. To meet such views it is necessary that our economic structure should have a gold *façade* in order to impress the uninitiated, but it is also very desirable that this *façade* should be supported by a structure fabricated of stronger materials than those of which it has been constructed in the past, and this aspect of the matter is of special importance when we come to consider the position as it actually exists at the present time.

The present is always the stepping-stone between the past and the future, but, however clearly we may discern the goal which we desire to reach, it is not always possible to effect an immediate transition to the newer and happier state towards which we wish to bend our footsteps. We have to consider therefore, not only the form which the monetary system should ultimately take, but also the arrangements which are necessary in order to facilitate the process of transition from the actual position of the moment to the better and more stable position which we wish to create.

The depression and the various developments which succeeded it have given rise to serious disequilibrium between the price levels of different countries, and the countries of the world are now divided into three monetary groups:—

(i) The sterling group, which has regained a certain measure of its lost prosperity by freeing itself from the trammels of the gold standard.

(ii) The gold *bloc*, which is committed to the policy of remaining on the gold standard.

(iii) The United States of America, which appears to be mainly dominated by the idea that the burden of internal debt should be lightened by raising the price level. Unfortunately the American Government has also taken up the attitude that it is justified in taking any steps whatever which can conceivably contribute to that end, irrespective of the effect which they may produce on international trade or on the monetary position of other countries. Among other things the gold parity of the dollar has been reduced to a figure which is definitely lower than that which would produce a position of equilibrium with the franc, and there is in consequence a constant drain of gold from Europe to America. Furthermore, a similar policy has been adopted in regard to silver and has caused a great deal of financial trouble in China.

Now it is clear that the policy of the gold *bloc* and the policy of the United States are mutually incompatible, and that no international monetary system can remain stable until such fundamental differences in outlook are removed. Even if temporary equilibrium is obtained by devaluation of the gold currencies, the adjustment will probably be followed in due course by a further devaluation of the dollar and the whole business of adjustment and re-adjustment will then start over again.

Permanent equilibrium requires that the countries of the gold *bloc* should recognise that a fixed attachment between the currency and gold is no longer practicable; but realisation of this truth will probably take years. It requires further that the United States should be brought to understand that monetary policies which cause harm to other countries can only lead to a succession of financial upheavals and the final disappearance of the

American export trade; but it is unlikely that this truth will be fully realised within the next decade.

The question arises therefore, can anything be done to expedite a general international acceptance of these simple economic facts? The question is very largely a political one and is evidently both difficult and controversial, but the author would venture to offer a suggestion which he feels might perhaps be accepted both by the gold *bloc* and by the United States. The suggestion is that the output of new gold should be rationed, and that each country should undertake not to make purchases of gold in the open market nor to accept transfers of gold from countries outside its own group in excess of its agreed allowance.

The chief advantage claimed for this scheme is that it is eminently reasonable and that there is some ground for hope that it might be accepted.

As regards the sterling group, the scheme would cause no inconvenience and acceptance could no doubt be taken for granted.

As regards the gold *bloc*, the scheme would have the great advantage that it would stop the excessive drain of gold from Europe to America which is such a serious source of weakness to the gold currencies at the present time. Furthermore, the checking of the outflow of gold would give to the Bank of England and the Bank of France, acting in combination, the power of controlling the price of gold on the London market and would thus make possible the restoration of equilibrium between sterling and the gold currencies. In return for these important advantages the countries of the gold *bloc* might be invited to adhere to the principle of the variable gold standard, and the co-operation of the sterling group might be made to depend on the acceptance of that condition.

As regards the United States, the effect of the scheme would be to bring into greater prominence the important question of controlling the trade balance, and this would be all to the good both for the United States itself and for the world at large.

To discuss this proposal in greater detail would, however, take us too far afield, and it is necessary to return to the main issue.

CHAPTER VIII

THE PROBLEM OF MANAGEMENT

CHARACTERISTICS OF A SUITABLE INSTRUMENT

THE problem of discovering suitable instruments of management for the control of national and international business relationships is evidently of fundamental importance, and many aspects of the question have attracted considerable attention, but I am not aware that anyone has attempted to define the characteristics by which the ideal instrument should be distinguished.

In the absence of any adequate previous investigation of this problem one is compelled to proceed with a certain amount of caution, and it is with due reserve that I suggest that the selection of a suitable instrument of management should be based on the following principles:—

(i) To be effective an instrument of management should act directly on the factor which it is desired to control.

As an example of the application of this principle, it must be noted that the management of the volume of credit is not a suitable instrument for the control of either the price level or the trade balance because it acts directly on the activity of trade, and its influence on the price level is only a secondary effect, while its influence on the trade balance is remoter still.

For the same reason the power to vary the gold parity of the currency cannot be regarded as a suitable instrument for the control of prices, for the reason that there is nowadays very little direct connection between the gold parity and the price level. Such connection as does exist arises mainly as an indirect effect which is due to the relationship which exists between the gold parity and the trade balance on the one hand and between foreign trade and home prices on the other.

(ii) Separate instruments of management are needed for each economic factor which it is desired to control.

The significance of this second principle has already been discussed in Chapter I. Its application to our search for an appropriate instrument for the control of the price level makes it necessary to exclude both the management of credit and variations in the gold parity (or the exchanges). The former is needed for controlling the activity of trade, and the latter for controlling the trade balance.

(iii) Provided that it satisfies the two primary requirements set forth above, the best instrument of management is the one which is easiest to administer and which involves the least possible interference in matters of detail. This aspect of the matter has been discussed by the author elsewhere. (10)

SHORT PERIOD MANAGEMENT

In our discussion on monetary theory in Chapter VI the conclusion was reached that there is no known means of controlling the price level over the short period. Rapid deflation cannot be brought about by any method at present known, and rapid inflation can only be brought about by destroying the confidence of the public. Once started this latter process is apt to get beyond control, and in any case it sets up all kinds of undesirable reactions. A mechanism of this type is quite unsuitable for the purpose of management.

Under normal conditions there is no known method of controlling the short period trend of prices, and under such conditions management is impossible.

MEDIUM PERIOD MANAGEMENT

Our policy in regard to any matter must necessarily depend to some extent on the efficiency of the instruments which are available for its realisation. It is merely futile to discuss ideals unless we can devise means for attaining them, and this, so it seems to me, is where many well-known writers on monetary policy have gone astray.

They assume, I think rightly, that the correct policy in regard to the (medium period) price level is stabilisation of prices, and they then assume, apparently without any adequate justification, that in either the management of credit or the variation of the gold parity there exists an instrument which will enable that policy to be made effective. The result has been that recent attempts to stabilise prices have only resulted in increasing the severity of the fluctuations which it was hoped to reduce.

It would seem then that it is necessary to make a different approach to the whole problem. It is clear that variations in the price level do occur and that they are due to a variety of causes. But we must accept the fact that we possess no instrument of management sufficiently powerful to override all adverse influences, and it is not possible therefore to control the price level after the manner in which the trade balance can be controlled by varying the exchanges. What then can be done?

Our objective is stabilisation of the price level. If we cannot control prices it is at least possible to avoid any course of action which is calculated to disturb them. Let us take in turn therefore each factor which is known to influence the price level, and let us consider what can be done to control it in such fashion that prices will not be too seriously disturbed.

THE ACTIVITY OF TRADE AND THE PRICE LEVEL

Expanding trade involves both increasing consumption and increasing production, but the former tends to lead, and expanding trade creates therefore a tendency towards rising prices. Stability of prices requires that the activity of trade should exhibit a uniform rate of progress, and that alternating booms and depressions should be avoided as far as possible.

Now the recognised instrument for controlling the activity of trade is the management of credit, and it is, I think, pretty generally agreed that it should be employed in such a way as to reduce the intensity of the fluctuations to which the activity of trade is liable under present conditions. The trouble is that unfortunately the art of management has not yet reached that state of perfection which is necessary in order to bring these disturbances under complete control.

However, that is another story. The immediate point is that any success which may be attained in subduing fluctuations in the activity of trade will also assist in the attainment of our objective of stabilising prices. If then we agree that the management of credit is to be employed in such a fashion that fluctuations in the activity of trade are reduced as far as possible, we thereby adopt the best possible policy for stabilising prices, and more than this is not possible.

WAGES AND THE PRICE LEVEL

Wages are the basis of all costs, and changes in rates of wages almost invariably lead, sooner or later, to corresponding changes in prices.

Orthodox theory, based on the monetary system

of the nineteenth century, required that prices should be flexible in order to secure control of the trade balance, and that wages should be flexible in order to secure flexibility of prices, and it is clear that this attitude is incompatible with modern views on the stabilisation of the price level.

In order to overcome this difficulty, it is necessary to accept the principle that the trade balance must be controlled by management of the exchanges, and, as soon as this point is conceded, stabilisation of prices becomes a perfectly practicable and reasonable policy. Stabilisation of wages also follows, and is in fact desirable in itself for other reasons. (11)

THE DEPRESSED INDUSTRIES AND THE PRICE LEVEL

From time to time inventions are made which increase the efficiency of some particular industry. If demand is elastic, a reduction in price may enable the additional output to be absorbed, and employment may remain unaffected. On the other hand, if demand is inelastic, consumption may fail to respond to the permissible reduction in price, and the industry will then pass into a state of unemployment and depression. This is what happened to agriculture in the United States and elsewhere in the years preceding the recent crisis, and the difficulties which arose from the over-production of wheat and the reactions which were produced thereby did much to provoke and accentuate that catastrophe.

Depression in a particular industry may well involve a serious fall in the price of the commodity concerned, and this is more especially the case when a lack of elasticity in demand is combined with highly competitive conditions in regard to production. Consequently, if an important industry becomes depressed and suffers from a fall in prices, there will result a corresponding fall in the price level as a whole. Complete stabilisation of prices involves, therefore, some adequate and satisfactory method of arranging for the transfer of surplus personnel from depressed trades to those which display greater opportunities for expansion.

The problem which thus arises is of very great importance, but it lies beyond the scope of the present essay.

THE VOLUME OF MONEY AND THE PRICE LEVEL

The quantity theory of money was discussed in Chapter VI, and it was pointed out that the influence exercised by the quantity of money on the price level is no longer direct, as it used to be before the evolution of the banking system. Nowadays the volume of cash has no direct influence on the price level, but such relationship as does exist arises out of the banker's liability to pay his depositors in cash, and is due to the fact that lack of cash may induce the central bank to contract credit and depress trade, while an excess of cash may lead to the development of a boom.

Experience shows that restrictions on the quantity of money may be a serious handicap to expanding trade, while an excessive supply of money may produce instability and subsequent collapse, and it is sometimes argued therefore that money should be neutral. The suggestion is eminently reasonable, and is in fact one of the conditions which must evidently be complied with if we are to secure stability of prices.

There is, however, a difficulty. The practical steps which must be taken in order that money shall be neutral are by no means obvious, and the whole question is a difficult and controversial one. It is proposed to return to the matter in the next Chapter.

LONG PERIOD MANAGEMENT

The question of policy was discussed in Chapter IV, and the conclusion was reached that the best policy for the long period is to aim at stability of commodity prices and a rising standard of wages. It was further suggested that the rate of increase in the average rate of wages should be approximately equal to the rate of increase in the efficiency of production, a quantity which was estimated at about 2 per cent. per annum.

At this point, however, it is necessary to refer to another factor in our problem.

What are generally called social services have now become an important feature in the economic structure and these payments form what is in effect an invisible addition to the actual rate of wages. Now it will be remembered that our agreed objective is the stabilisation of commodity prices, and before deciding on the wage policy which is calculated to bring about this result it is clearly necessary to make allowance for this invisible increase. The writer has made no attempt to determine the actual increase in costs which has been produced in recent years by this invisible addition to wages, and it is only possible to deal with the matter on a purely hypothetical basis. (12)

Assume, for example, that provision for social services is increasing and that it is adding 1 per cent. to the average cost of production; assume further that the standard of living is rising at the rate of 2 per cent. per annum. Then it is clear that the increase in the average rate of wages which would correspond with the stabilisation of commodity prices would in that case be 1 per cent. per annum.

THE AVERAGE RATE OF WAGES AS AN INSTRUMENT OF MANAGEMENT

We now arrive at the most important and at the same time the most controversial aspect of our problem—the selection of a suitable instrument for the control of the long period price level, and it is necessary to begin by eliminating certain methods which have been suggested but which do not comply with our requirements.

It has been suggested, for example, that the bank rate and other recognised expedients for controlling credit should be made use of for the control of the price level, but the proposal is open to the following objections:—

(i) The relationship between the price level and the volume of credit is not sufficiently direct to form a satisfactory basis for a system of management.

(ii) The management of credit is required as an instrument for the more important purpose of controlling the activity of trade and should not therefore be regarded as available for any other purpose.

(iii) The policy in question was tried in Great Britain from 1920 onwards and was found to be disastrous. (13) It may also be mentioned that stabilisation of prices by means of credit control has always been popular in the United States, and there is little doubt that this attitude helped to influence the abnormal expansion of credit which occurred in 1928. In short the scheme has been tried in practice and found wanting.

It has also been suggested that a change in the price level may be brought about by altering the gold parity of the currency, and no doubt there was a time when such an expedient might have been effective. Under modern conditions, however, the position is different, and the scheme is open to the following objections:—

(i) People no longer think in terms of gold but in terms of pounds, dollars, francs or whatever it may be, and there exists therefore no direct relationship between the gold parity and the price level.

(ii) The gold parity has a much more powerful influence on the trade balance than it has on the price level, and it should be regarded as the appropriate instrument of management for the control of the former and not of the latter.

(iii) Recent attempts to utilise the gold parity of the dollar as an instrument for raising prices in the United States have not yielded the desired results and have confirmed the conclusions set forth above; in so far as any success has been attained it may well be attributed to other causes.

Yet another instrument for controlling the price level is sometimes suggested and that is the management of the volume of money, and here one must distinguish between the conditions which prevailed in former centuries and the conditions of to-day. Before the development of the banking system the relationship between the volume of money and the price level was much more direct than it is now. At the present day the volume of money has a slow and somewhat uncertain influence on the credit policy of the central bank, the policy of the central bank has a slow and uncertain influence on the activity of trade, and the activity of trade has a slow and very uncertain influence on the price level. If the management of credit is a slow and clumsy instrument for the control of the price level, then *a fortiori* we must condemn the proposal that the volume of money should be regarded as a suitable instrument for this purpose.

We are therefore constrained to reject all the instruments of management which have hitherto been proposed for the management of the price level, and it becomes necessary to examine this very important and controversial problem *de novo.* The solution which the author would venture to put forward for consideration is simply this:—

The average rate of wages has a direct influence on prices and may be regarded as a suitable and appropriate instrument for the control of the price level.

Let us consider therefore what arguments can be suggested in favour of this proposal and what objections may be urged against it.

The first and most important point in favour of the proposal is that wages are an essential item in the cost of every important commodity and every important service, and that there is therefore a direct and positive relationship between the rate of wages and the price level. It is for this reason especially that the proposed instrument may be expected to succeed where other systems have failed. The presumption is of course that the employer of labour will be left free to fix his selling price on the basis of his costs exactly as he does at present. Under normal conditions the manufacturer will protect his own interests and will take care not to fix the price too low. On the other hand, the problem of preventing excessive profits and of guarding the consumer against excessive prices will remain unaffected, except in so far as it will be simplified by the general atmosphere of stability which should result from properly organised and effective management.

A second important consideration is that the instrument of management is not needed for other purposes.

A third and incidental but not unimportant advantage is that the scheme would do much to reduce the friction which often arises at the present time between employers and employed over the question of wages. The great difficulty in these disputes is that there are no accepted principles in accordance with which a just and reasonable settlement can be arrived at. The judge or arbitrator has to make up his own mind whether, in making his award, he will be guided by the wages actually being paid in other industries, or whether he must consider the extent of unemployment or the magnitude of the profits or losses of the employer. In actual practice, however, he will probably ignore all these considerations and give an award which both sides seem likely to accept. If the proposed scheme is adopted, however, there seems to be good reason to hope that it will form the basis of a wages system which will enable any disputed point to be settled *on the basis of agreed principles* by any joint committee of employers and employed.

As regards possible disadvantages the chief objection which may be urged against the scheme is,

I think, that it is easy to alter wages upwards but much more difficult to alter them downwards.

It will be remarked, however, that we have decided in favour of a stable price level and that we have pointed out that this policy is likely to involve an increase in the average rate of wages of the order of 1 or 2 per cent. per annum. In dealing with individual cases it is possible therefore to confine any alterations between the limit of no change on the one hand and increases up to say 5 per cent. per annum on the other. In other words, it should be possible to secure adequate flexibility without any downward adjustments at all.

Another argument which may be put forward is that the ideal of a stable price level may be unattainable, that events abroad, or the requirements of the trade balance may render such an ideal impracticable. In answer to this objection it must be pointed out that the argument is based upon a condition of affairs which has existed in the past but which need not exist in the future. The policy of deflating prices has been adopted in the past either because it was believed that a reduction of prices was desirable in itself, or else because it was necessary in order to control the balance of trade. The first of these points has already been dealt with in Chapter IV. As regards the control of the trade balance the author contends that the desire to deflate prices in order to bring about an adjustment of the trade balance arises from an obsolete and fallacious monetary theory. In a more enlightened world the trade balance will be controlled by managing the exchanges and the need for deflation will not arise.

THE WAGES BOARD

The question of the approved policy in regard to the price level, and of the corresponding increase in the average rate of wages which is believed to be appropriate in order to make that policy effective, must first be decided on. Let it be assumed for the sake of argument that it is decided to raise the average rate of wages at the rate of 2 per cent. per annum. Then it is necessary to arrange that effect should be given to that decision.

Perhaps the reader has been drifting unconsciously towards the view that it is merely necessary to raise wages all round at the rate of 2 per cent. per annum, but that is not the author's view at all. There are other important aspects of the matter to be considered.

In the first place there will always be particular trades which consider that they are worse off than their neighbours and that their case needs special consideration. The power of the Wages Board to accord special treatment to particular trades will enable it to set right any legitimate grievances.

In the second place there is the problem of the declining trades, or perhaps it would be more correct to describe it as the problem of transferring capital and labour from old trades to new ones. And one of the most serious difficulties in providing for such changes is the reluctance of individuals to change their trade and to change their place of residence. It is necessary that they should be offered some countervailing attraction to induce them to do so, and an appropriate policy in regard to wages would seem to provide the required incentive. In the case of the declining trades the Wages Board would encourage workers to leave by refusing any increase of wages, and in the case of the expanding trades wage-earners would be attracted by the inducement of wages which were above the average. The proposed system if properly used, therefore, would place in the hands of the Wages Board a powerful and convenient instrument for controlling the distribution of labour.

The question of the composition of the Wages Board need not detain us since any representative body of employers and employed should have no difficulty in dealing with the problems which would arise. Their deliberations would be enormously simplified owing to the fact that they would be acting on definite and clearly defined principles, whereas in the past the adjustment of wages has simply been a question of hard bargaining, and the arbitrators have been more concerned with the question of finding a solution which both sides would be prepared to accept than in considering any merits which the case might be supposed to possess.

As regards the powers which would be given to the Wages Board, a large degree of freedom would no doubt be desirable in dealing with particular cases, but the powers of the Board would be definitely limited by the condition that the increase in the average rate of wages should not exceed 2 per cent. or whatever the authorised figure might be. Within this limit the Board would be allowed as wide a discretion as possible.

THE EMERGENCY CONTROL OF PRICES

The situation in the United States of America in recent years has presented for solution an emergency problem of great interest and importance. During the early years of the crisis there was a serious fall in the general level of prices, and it was conceived to be necessary that the price level should be raised in order to bring about a more reasonable position as between debtor and creditor. Orthodox economic theory offers no adequate solution to this problem, and various emergency measures of an admittedly experimental character were tried, but they have only been partially successful in securing the results which have been aimed at.

While it is difficult to speak with confidence in regard to an untried expedient, the author believes that the most promising method for dealing with a situation of this character would be to pass a law raising all wages and salaries in a certain proportion on a certain date. So far as trade and industry are concerned business men would then be left free to raise prices by appropriate amounts which would vary in each particular case but which would never exceed the proportion already fixed in the case of wages. As regards the budget certain taxes would remain unaffected while certain others would need alteration, but the principles involved present no particular difficulty.

There have of course been other problems to deal with in the United States besides this matter of the price level, and the whole situation has been extremely complex, but these other matters do not appear to affect the validity of the present argument. In so far as it was thought desirable to raise the price level, the suggestion is that wages should be raised in some definite proportion, and that the economic structure should then be left to adjust itself to the new conditions. It is submitted that this method of dealing with the problem would be more effective and would cause less objectionable reactions than any of the methods actually adopted.

In other words, the suggestion is that a controlled inflation (or reflation if the expression is preferred) of specified amount can be brought about more readily and effectively by raising wages than by any other method which has been tried or suggested.

CHAPTER IX

THE MANAGEMENT OF CREDIT

THE EFFECT OF BETTER CONTROL

THE adoption of additional instruments of control to supplement the management of credit will necessarily have a vital influence on the whole art of management. If the utmost advantage is to be secured from the introduction of a new and better system, it is necessary that the principles which have hitherto guided central banks in the management of credit should be reviewed, and that a new technique of management should be developed which will be consistent in itself and which will make the best possible use of the new instruments.

THE PATTERN OF PRODUCTION

The field of industry may be likened to a carpet in which various coloured threads are woven together in certain proportions, and it is necessary that these proportions should be correctly determined in order that actual production should be in agreement with consumers' demand. The quantity of any particular thread which is required depends both upon the size of the carpet and its pattern, and the producer of that particular thread has to take both these factors into consideration in making his arrangements for future production.

An increase in the size of the population involves merely an increase in the size of the carpet, but an improved standard of living involves not only an increase in the volume but also a change in the pattern of consumption, and it is these changes in the pattern which render the forecasting of demand so extremely difficult and uncertain.

It is a paradox of the modern economic structure that there are occasions when a lack of purchasing power among millions of people is to be found at a time when there exist large stocks of goods which the market is unable to absorb, and that idle factories and a high proportion of unemployed are also symptoms of these particular periods. Unfortunately the granting of additional purchasing power to the unemployed would not solve the problem, for they would not demand the particular goods which happen to be surplus nor those which the idle factories are capable of producing. It is the pattern of production which has gone wrong, and further progress is not possible until it is put right again.

Now the rate at which changes are brought about in consumers' demand and in the corresponding pattern of production is limited by various factors which are not under control. There is a limit set by the rate at which new inventions can be developed and put into use, by the rate at which the habits of individual people can be changed, by the rate at which people can be displaced from old industries and absorbed into new ones, and so on. If an attempt is made to force the pace, the pattern of consumers' demand and the pattern of production get out of adjustment with the actual situation which has been created by the optimism of producers, and there ensues an accumulation of unsaleable goods or the creation of unwanted factories, and a realisation of the true position leads eventually to collapse and depression.

Situations of this type give rise to problems of two distinct types in the art of management. Firstly, there is the problem of managing the total volume of credit so as to check over-expansion when there is evidence that the economic structure is becoming unstable. Secondly, there is the problem of facilitating the transfer of capital and labour from old and declining industries to new and expanding ones.

THE USE OF CREDIT FOR THE CONTROL OF THE ACTIVITY OF TRADE

As already pointed out in the preceding section, it is one of the functions of management to arrange matters so that the rate of expansion of the activity of trade shall be the highest which is possible without running the risk of instability and subsequent collapse. This is the primary function of credit control, and is the function for which credit control was originally developed. It was only at a later stage that central banks, owing to the lack of any other instrument of management, were compelled to employ the management of credit for the control of the trade balance and the price level.

Under a new and better system of management we are entitled to assume that the complications which are liable to arise owing to a lack of balance between imports and exports, or owing to serious fluctuations in prices, are brought under reasonable control by the methods already referred to, and that the management of credit can be used exclusively for its original and legitimate purpose. That is to say, restriction of credit will be resorted to whenever it is clear that industry is exhibiting a tendency to expand too rapidly and that the pattern of production is not adapting itself to the pattern of consumption, but it will not be used for any other reason. It will no longer be necessary to create artificial depressions in trade and industry in accordance with the dictates of a false and obsolete monetary theory. The question then arises:

How is it possible to know that the pattern of production and the pattern of consumption are drifting out of adjustment and that the application of restrictive measures is desirable?

It is of vital importance that this question should be answered correctly, but the whole matter is evidently difficult and controversial, and it is not to be expected that a completely satisfactory solution can be arrived at without a certain amount of trial and error. Some of the various aspects of the problem are discussed in the following sections.

A RISING PRICE LEVEL AS AN INDICATION OF BOOM CONDITIONS

In certain stages of a boom, labour and the other factors of production may be fully employed, at least in particular industries, and shortage of supplies may lead to rising prices. It may be said therefore that high or rising prices are an indication of boom conditions and low or falling prices of slump conditions, and there is certainly some truth to be found in such statements. Recent experience has tended to show, however, that the reactions involved are not reliable, and that the price level does not invariably respond in the manner which this simple theory would lead us to expect. In the United States the 1928 boom, which immediately preceded the recent crisis, was not accompanied by any very conspicuous rise in prices. Again, in the decade which preceded Great Britain's departure from the gold standard, there was a serious decline in the activity of trade, but no decline of prices of similar importance.

We must conclude then, that under modern conditions, the price level is not a reliable indicator of the activity of trade. We cannot conclude with certainty that rising prices indicate a boom, and still less can we conclude, and this is really the important point, that stable prices are an indication that boom conditions are absent.

A SHORTAGE OF CASH AS AN INDICATION OF BOOM CONDITIONS

Expanding trade involves a greater use of money of all kinds and bankers are in practice compelled to take this fact into account. They are legally obliged to pay their depositors in cash, and failure to discharge this obligation involves a breakdown of the whole monetary system. If the central bank foresees that the demand for cash is likely to become excessive it restricts credit in order to bring about a restriction of demand.

Now the shortage of cash may be due to the existence of boom conditions, and in that case the action of the bank may be beneficial; it may check the boom and may thereby reduce the severity of the subsequent collapse. On the other hand, a shortage of cash may arise in circumstances which do not correspond with boom conditions at all, and in that case restriction of credit creates an artificial depression which is very undesirable and quite unnecessary. It is necessary to ask therefore, in the long run is the policy of restricting the volume of cash desirable or not?

I suppose that the majority of economists would answer this question by pointing out that such a policy has produced satisfactory results in the past, and with this statement the author is disposed to agree. It is also not unreasonable to argue that some restriction of the volume of cash may still be employed with beneficial effects.

But if it is contended that the volume of cash should be fixed and invariable or that it should be made to depend on the volume of gold which the banks happen to be able to acquire, then the writer is compelled to place on record his minute of dissent. The only form of policy which can be logically justified is one based on the principle that money should be neutral, that is to say the volume of money must be allowed to expand at whatever rate is necessary in order to keep pace with the normal expansion of business.

Assuming, and it is perhaps rather a large assumption, that the correct volume of cash corresponding to some particular set of conditions can be determined, provision should then be made for expansion to allow for increases in the population and for a rising standard of living. On the other hand, the increasing use of cheques reduces the need for cash, and, if the tendency is sufficiently pronounced, it might be necessary to allow for this factor also. The matter is not without difficulty, but it seems reasonable to assume that any factor which is of sufficient importance to be significant can be estimated and allowed for, and that it is possible to devise a formula which would enable the appropriate changes in the volume of cash to be decided on with sufficient accuracy for practical purposes.

It is therefore possible, I think, to justify the

conclusion that some system for regulating the volume of cash may well serve a useful purpose, and a shortage of cash may then be regarded as a helpful indication, in conjunction with other known methods, that restriction of credit should be seriously considered.

THE DEMAND FOR CREDIT AS AN INDICATION OF BOOM CONDITIONS

Unsaleable goods must necessarily be financed by someone, and special demands for credit in order to carry abnormal stocks are a well-known symptom of boom conditions. It is true that these signs become most apparent when the boom has already reached its zenith, but they can hardly be entirely absent in the early stages, and their appearance should not be overlooked. An accumulation of abnormal stocks of wheat, for example, was one of the characteristic symptoms which made itself apparent in the years preceding the recent depression, and the demand for financial accommodation to finance these abnormal stocks should certainly have been regarded as a danger signal.

AN ABNORMAL INCREASE IN THE VOLUME OF DEBT AS AN INDICATION OF BOOM CONDITIONS

If money is lent in order to facilitate the expansion of trade and industry, and if the expansion in the value of real assets keeps pace with the expansion of debt, the whole business is perfectly legitimate and reasonable. But if the volume of debt in a community increases more rapidly than the value of the real assets, then there is a definite danger that the burden of debt will become intolerable and the progress of trade and industry will be impeded. An increasing burden of debt may be caused by efforts to finance too rapid an expansion of industry, by borrowing to support depressed industries with an inelastic market (such as agriculture), by excessive speculation in stocks and shares, by falling prices and so on, but, however produced, the general effects which result from an excessive burden of debt are equally undesirable.

In recent years the United States of America has suffered from a phenomenal fall in prices to which all the above factors appear to have contributed to a greater or less extent. The result has been that a policy of raising prices by any and every means available has definitely dominated the monetary actions of the American Government. Many economists would disagree no doubt with some of the steps which have been taken with a view to raising prices, but few would take exception to the statement that the rising burden of debt has been a serious source of embarrassment.

It must be remembered that debt and credit are simply different names for the same transaction viewed from the different viewpoints of borrower and lender respectively, and the existence of a large burden of debt is evidently a sound reason for avoiding any course of action which might tend to increase it.

As soon as it becomes evident that debt is increasing more rapidly than the value of the real assets which it was incurred to finance, then the case for restricting credit is clear.

THE DISTRIBUTION OF CREDIT BETWEEN DIFFERENT INDUSTRIES

The march of progress makes it inevitable that new industries should appear and expand and that old industries should decline and disappear, and the process involves the transfer of both labour and capital from the old industries to the new.

To some extent economic forces exist which tend to bring about the necessary transfer, but they act too slowly. The problem of devising some adequate scheme for expediting the transfer of labour and capital from old to new industries is one of the most pressing problems of national planning which faces us at the present day. To a great extent the problem is one which lies beyond the scope of our present inquiry, but it is legitimate to ask: What is the correct credit policy to adopt in regard to depressed industries?

It will often be found that the equipment of a depressed industry has been allowed to deteriorate, and that demands are made for rationalisation and cheap credit with which the proposed reorganisation may be effected. But is the provision of cheap credit the proper course?

New and expanding industries do not ask for cheap credit for they get all the money they want without difficulty. The reason an industry cannot borrow is that its prospects are regarded unfavourably by those who are best qualified to judge, and it may be said with a fair degree of certainty that the lack of cheap credit is never the chief cause of depression in any particular industry.

Moreover, if credits are provided without removing the fundamental causes of the depression they are only likely to make matters worse. They may be frittered away on trying to bolster up an impossible position and may only serve to drive the original proprietors of industry more surely along the road to bankruptcy. Or they may be used to increase the efficiency of production and thereby increase the glut of commodities in an inelastic and already overcrowded market.

Appeals for cheap credit from some industry are usually distress signals caused by over-production and should always be looked upon with suspicion.

In such cases the real choice to be made by the community lies between two alternatives. Either the industry must be allowed to decline and the transfer of surplus personnel to other industries must be facilitated, or else the industry must be maintained at an artificial level by subsidies in one form or another. In such schemes credit facilities may play a necessary part, but special credit facilities should never be regarded as a panacea for depression in individual industries, which is of course quite a different matter from the question of keeping down the cost of credit to industry as a whole.

THE ART OF MANAGEMENT

It may be said with a considerable amount of truth that the management of credit is an art and that art knows no rules, and the remarks made in the preceding sections are merely intended to direct attention to some of the factors which would be taken into account in making an appreciation of the situation. The evolution of a suitable technique would come with experience, and the policy of the currency authority would no doubt be guided by the following principles:—

Firstly, the aim of management should be to keep the rate of interest as low as possible.

Secondly, restriction should be applied when there is reason to believe that expansion is proceeding too rapidly, but not otherwise.

Thirdly, when action is necessary it should be taken as quickly as possible. As soon as it becomes clear that there exists a serious lack of adjustment in any direction and that restriction of credit will ultimately be necessary, it should be applied as rapidly as possible: delay only aggravates the trouble and intensifies the ensuing depression.

CHAPTER X

CONCLUSION

CONSISTENCY IN ECONOMIC POLICIES

One of the greatest obstacles which lie in the way of any improvement in the international monetary situation at the present time lies in the inability of the average citizen to realise that certain policies are mutually inconsistent, and that attempts to pursue two inconsistent policies at the same time only cause confusion and hinder the process of recovery instead of assisting it.

The various creditor nations are particularly to blame in this respect. They demand payment from their foreign debtors and at the same time adopt measures which effectually prevent the creation of a balance of imports by means of which the debt could be paid. The private citizen is told that foreign countries have defaulted and refused to pay their debts, whereas in fact it is the government of the creditor country which has determined the magnitude of the payment, but has not been sufficiently honest or courageous to accept responsibility for its own actions.

And this same problem of the trade balance leads to another form of inconsistency. Interest on foreign loans is payable in the form of an excess of imports over exports, while an expansion of exports serves, temporarily at least, to reduce unemployment. But do the governments of creditor countries make an honest attempt to face this question and strike a fair balance between the rival claimants? I fear not; it is so much easier to avoid the issue and pretend that both claims can be satisfied in full.

Yet another aspect of the problem arises in connection with the use of protectionist tariffs. The writer has pointed out elsewhere (14) that a system of tariffs cannot be varied sufficiently rapidly to enable it to be regarded as a suitable instrument for the control of the trade balance. A system of tariffs must rather be regarded as an instrument for controlling the volume of foreign trade. If imports are restricted, exports must, after a short period of adjustment, fall also. Yet what government which advocates a restriction of imports is prepared to confess that its policy is one of restricting exports? Does it not rather try to disguise the unpleasant fact that a reduction of imports and an expansion of exports are two policies which are mutually inconsistent?

A further example of this type of error is to be found among those who support a return to the fixed gold standard and who in the next breath advocate the stabilisation of prices. Yet it has been known for more than a century that the proper working of the fixed gold standard involves changes in the price level including changes in wages. (15)

But it is unnecessary to add to the list. It is only

possible to repeat that unless a policy is consistent in itself it can lead nowhere.

MONETARY SYSTEMS OLD AND NEW

It is convenient to summarise in this final chapter the general argument which is set forth in the preceding pages and in the writer's earlier book *The Trade Balance*, for these two books should be regarded as dealing with distinct but complementary aspects of a single monetary system.

The starting-point of the argument is the fact that the monetary system of the nineteenth century has broken down, and it is suggested further that the failure is beyond repair, that the older system is no longer workable, and that a new and more elaborate system is necessary to meet the more exacting requirements of the present day.

Perhaps the writer's attitude in regard to this matter may be made clearer by means of an analogy.

Let us compare the monetary system of the nineteenth century to a transport system such as the railways or the trams in which each vehicle is designed to run on rails which entirely control the direction of its movements. In such systems the vehicle itself needs only one type of control, a control to regulate the *speed*. And so it was with the nineteenth-century monetary system; only one form of control was necessary, and this control took the form of controlling the volume of credit by means of the bank rate.

Nowadays transport is no longer confined to vehicles running on rails. The first step was the introduction of motor-cars which are designed to move on any flat surface. Such vehicles require two types of control, the one to regulate the *speed* and the other to regulate the *direction*. The next step was the introduction of the aeroplane, which is not constrained to move on the surface of the ground, and which requires three types of control to regulate *speed*, *direction* and *height* respectively.

And so it is with the monetary system, conditions have changed, a single instrument of control is no longer adequate, and at least three instruments of control are now required if the control of the system is to be effective.

The three principal factors which need control in the monetary system are *the activity of trade*, *the trade balance* and *the price level*, and it has been the purpose of these essays to discuss the various instruments which are available and to select those which are most appropriate for each particular purpose.

THE ORTHODOX POSITION

There are many financiers and economists, belonging to what I may call the extreme orthodox school, who believe that an attempt should be made to restore the fixed gold standard of the nineteenth century, and this proposal raises two questions, How is it proposed to control the trade balance? and How is it proposed to control the price level?

After the recent crash, which arose largely from failure to control the trade balances, it can hardly be suggested that the trade balance can be left to look after itself, and the orthodox reply is that the flow of trade induces a flow of gold in the opposite direction, that the flow of gold causes an internal adjustment of prices and that the changes in prices bring about an adjustment of the trade balance.

Those who believe that this mechanism is still workable should read chapter five of *The Great Depression*. The chapter in question deals with the position in Great Britain in 1931 when the high price level had led to a serious adverse balance of trade, and in it Prof. Robbins sets forth the orthodox view of the situation. In spite of the fact that there were at the time over two million unemployed, the orthodox policy would have involved an increase of the bank rate in the hope that further restriction of trade would ultimately correct the trade balance by means of a general fall in wages and prices.

The present writer does not know what Prof. Robbins' personal views may be nor what impression the chapter in question may create in the minds of other readers, but in his own mind it has certainly conjured up the picture of an able and conscientious advocate who is painfully aware of the weakness of his own case. He has dealt with the matter more fully elsewhere. (16)

SOME UNORTHODOX VIEWS

The need for securing some sort of control over the trade balance has led to various systems of exchange control and to the adoption of bilateral agreements between certain countries, and there are some enthusiasts who go so far as to suggest that these devices should be made permanent. In practice, however, such arrangements constitute a very serious handicap to international trade, and it is certain that they would be abolished to-morrow if the necessary balance between imports and exports could be secured in any other way.

Turning to other unorthodox schools of thought, there are a number of writers on economic and monetary theory who have expressed the belief that the chief cause of industrial depressions is the restriction of credit, and who have evolved various systems for removing this defect. It is not necessary to discuss these schemes in detail as they all appear to be open to objections of one sort or another. There is no smoke without fire, however, and the writer has been driven to the conclusion that, on the main issue, the unorthodox critics are right and the orthodox school of bankers and economists is wrong.

History tells us that there have been periods of over-investment and that there have been periods of over-trading, and experience shows that restriction of credit under such conditions is beneficial and tends to modify the intensity of the inevitable reaction. But there is no other justification for restricting credit and hampering the activity of trade. For example, restriction of credit was not justified in Great Britain in 1924 and still less would it have been justified in 1931.

But the believers in cheap credit are not the only critics of orthodoxy: there is also a school which believes in the stabilisation of prices. Many of these people go too far: they assume that absolute stabilisation is possible (which is untrue), and they suggest methods for attaining their objective which are open to serious criticism. But modify the doctrine so as to meet these criticisms and say simply that prices should be stabilised as far as possible; how does this affect the position?

The orthodox school cannot accept price stabilisation even in this modified form, for the proper working of the fixed gold standard requires that prices and wages should be flexible. Here again I suggest that the orthodox school is wrong, and that the unorthodox school is right, at least up to a point.

THE TRADE BALANCE

If it has done nothing else the great depression has compelled national governments to take notice of the trade balance and to take steps of one sort or another for its control. It is fairly obvious that the emergency measures adopted are very unsatisfactory, and it is clearly desirable that they should be replaced as soon as possible by something better.

The writer has explained why a return to the fixed gold standard cannot provide a satisfactory solution to this problem, and has suggested that the proper instrument of control is a variable gold parity (or variable exchange parity).

In criticising this form of control, a friend remarked to the writer that an objection to the scheme was that it appeared to make currency depreciation respectable. Even assuming that world-wide adoption of the practice has not already made currency depreciation respectable, the writer is quite prepared to accept this phrase as a perfectly fair description of his intentions. At the same time it must be noted that it is not the act itself which is respectable or otherwise but the way in which it is carried out.

If I stick a knife into my neighbour in such a way as to cause bodily injury because I disagree with his opinions, then the act is highly improper. But if a properly qualified surgeon sticks a knife into his patient in the hope that the patient will ultimately benefit from the operation, the act is quite proper and entirely respectable. And so it is with currency depreciation: everything depends on the circumstances and on the skill with which the operation is performed. There is no reason why currency depreciation (or appreciation) should not be highly beneficial or why it should not be regarded as respectable, provided a proper technique is developed for its use, and provided the practice of the craft is left in skilled hands.

THE PRICE LEVEL

The first thing which must be decided in regard to the price level is whether the national policy is to involve stabilisation or not, and the position of the orthodox school in regard to this matter has already been pointed out.

Rejecting the orthodox view and adopting the view that prices should be stabilised as far as practicable, two questions remain to be settled: firstly, how far stabilisation is practicable, and secondly, what means are available for attaining this objective.

As regards the first question the author's investigation has led to the conclusion that price control over the short period is impracticable and that price control over the medium period is only practicable to a limited extent. It is only when we come to the long period trend of prices that a real choice of policy is available, and on this issue the author reaches the conclusion that stabilisation of commodity prices is the policy which appears to possess the balance of advantages.

As regards the means to be adopted for controlling the price level, the author argues that neither changes in the bank rate nor changes in the gold parity are either effective for the purpose or desirable in themselves, and suggests that the proper instrument of management is the average rate of wages. Details of the scheme have already been discussed and need not be repeated here.

THE POSITION OF GOLD AND SILVER

The author has endeavoured to show that the fixed gold standard of the nineteenth century is unworkable under modern conditions, but he has no desire to suggest that gold and silver will cease to play essential *rôles* in the monetary system of the future. The main difference will be that they will cease to be regarded as standards of value. In the monetary system of the future the trend of prices will be controlled, not by the uncertain balance between the supply and demand for gold, but by deliberate management on some such system as that foreshadowed in the preceding pages.

A second change will be in the position of gold and silver in relation to international trade. No scheme of management can be devised which will act instantaneously, and it is necessary that the system should contain in itself a certain inherent flexibility. During the nineteenth century that flexibility was secured partly by the flow of gold, and partly by the operations of the London money market and the British investor.

It is clear that gold and silver have still an important part to play in this regard, and it is certainly desirable that as large a proportion as possible of the world's monetary gold and silver should be rendered mobile so as to make them free to perform this important function. Incidentally it may be observed that the acceptance of the principle of the variable parity removes the century-old difficulty of running gold and silver in double harness, for it leaves the management free to adopt different rates for gold and silver and thereby makes possible the adjustment in relative prices which is necessary in order to allow for changes in the relative costs of production.

It is unlikely, however, that the volume of mobile gold and silver will ever be sufficiently great to provide adequate flexibility, and it is therefore clear that reserves of gold and silver will have to be supplemented by reserves of foreign paper of one form or another. In other words, the national reserves of the future will consist partly of gold and silver and partly of foreign paper, and will in fact bear a strong resemblance to the British exchange equalisation fund of the present day.

THE IMPORTANCE OF GREAT BRITAIN'S POSITION

The present monetary position of the world is one of very great difficulty and danger. There is the immediate problem of restoring equilibrium between the price levels of the three monetary groups into which the world is now divided, and there is the less urgent but perhaps more vital problem of devising an international monetary system which shall be stable in itself and which shall make possible a revival of international trade.

It is with this latter problem that the author has been mainly concerned both in this essay and its predecessor, and he has endeavoured to show that a new and better type of monetary system is practicable.

There are a great many people in Great Britain, however, including a number of those who are entitled to speak with authority on economic and monetary problems, who believe that a return to the fixed gold standard should be brought about at the earliest possible moment, and against this attitude the writer desires to enter a final protest.

In the first place there are reasons for believing that the fixed gold standard is inherently unstable and therefore unworkable under modern conditions, but this is not all. Both the gold *bloc* and the United States desire that there should be a return to the fixed gold standard, but their whole attitude towards such a system is fundamentally different. The gold *bloc* countries are inclined to worship gold in itself and to regard it as the one safe refuge against currency instability. On the other hand, the outstanding feature of recent events in the United States is the development of the idea that control of the price level should be regarded as the primary objective of monetary policy. The fixed gold standard is not regarded in the United States as a medium of international trade the successful working of which demands occasional sacrifice of what appear to be national interests. It is merely regarded as a fulcrum which can be made use of to bring pressure to bear on the internal price level.

Even if the system were inherently sound (which it is not) this fundamental difference of outlook would render impossible its successful operation for any prolonged period of time. There would be a temporary revival of international trade followed by a fresh collapse.

At the moment a return to the fixed gold standard is prevented by the existing disequilibrium of the price levels of the gold *bloc* on the one hand and the United States on the other, but at any moment the resistance of the gold *bloc* may be overcome and the course of international events will then depend upon the attitude of Great Britain.

The vital fact at the present time is that the sterling group still retains its freedom of action, and the way is still open for modifying and reforming the international monetary system in whatever way may be shown to be necessary or desirable. Once the sterling group returns to the fixed gold standard, however, vested interests are created and all freedom of action is lost. If once the irrevocable step is taken the commerce of the world will be bound in golden fetters from which it cannot be released save by the overwhelming pressure of a fresh crisis.

In this critical situation Great Britain has a

unique opportunity. She can refuse to be shackled and hindered any longer by the obsolete monetary system of the nineteenth century, and can insist that an attempt shall be made to establish a new system which shall be better adapted to the more exacting requirements of the present day.

REFERENCES

1. Sir C. Morgan-Webb: *The Rise and Fall of the Gold Standard* (1934), p. 53.

2. L. Robbins: *The Great Depression* (1934), p. 97.

3. K. E. Edgeworth: *The Trade Balance* (1934), chap. v.

4. ,, ,, : *The Industrial Crisis* (1933), chap. vi.

5. A similar conclusion is arrived at by a group of the Royal Institute for International Affairs in *The Future of Monetary Policy* (1935), p. 61.

6. J. M. Keynes: *A Treatise on Money* (1930), chap. 30.

7. Sir C. Morgan-Webb: *loc. cit.*, chap. iv.

8. K. E. Edgeworth: *The Industrial Crisis*, p. 129.

9. The view here expressed seems to be supported by the authors of *The Future of Monetary Policy*, p. 208.

10. K. E. Edgeworth: *The Trade Balance*, pp. 24–25.

11. ,, ,, : *The Industrial Crisis*, p. 91.

12. *The Economist*, 13th April 1935, supplement, p. 12, estimates that the value of social services has been offset by increased taxation of the wage-earning classes.

13. K. E. Edgeworth: *The Industrial Crisis*, chap. xvii.

14. ,, ,, : *The Trade Balance*, p. 55.

15. See, for example, Ricardo: *Principles of Political Economy and Taxation*, edited by E. C. K. Gonner, chap. vii.

16. K. E. Edgeworth: *The Trade Balance*, p. 71.

INDEX